Detoxifying the Culture

John A. Howard

With the warmest good wishes
to good friend, Shep

[signature]

4/17/02

AmErica House
Baltimore

First printing

ISBN: 1-58851-395-5
PUBLISHED BY AMERICA HOUSE BOOK PUBLISHERS
www.publishamerica.com
Baltimore

Printed in the United States of America

DETOXIFYING THE CULTURE

Table of Contents

Chapter IV
"How Did We Get Into This Mess"
Keynote Address for the Annual State Convention of the Arkansas
Farm Bureau at Little Rock, Arkansas
30 November 1978
An analysis of the damage done, when the purpose of the Federal
Government was transformed from protecting the citizens in the
proper activities of their daily life and protecting the nation from
foreign interference, to providing rights, privileges, benefits,
special protection and subsidies to competing interest groups.

Chapter V
"Legalized Gambling: A Foolish Bet"
Text of *Persuasion At Work*, a monthly newsletter published by
Rockford College
September 1979
The something-for-nothing mind-set induced by the welfare state,
institutionalized and rendered addictive by the hard-sell marketing
of state lotteries.

Chapter VI
"A Sure Compass: American Society Has Lost Its Sense of
Direction"
Address for the 25th Anniversary Banquet of *The St. Croix
Review* at St. Paul, Minnesota
21 October 1992
The attacks on standards of behavior by radical student groups,
and the amoral movies, books, and rock music, leading up to the
Woodstock festival and its massive public defiance of moral
standards and public law.

PREFACE

By Dr. Herbert I. London
President of the Hudson Institute

As Charles Dickens so aptly noted about the French Revolution: "These are the best of times and the worst of times." Surely the same can be said about our era.

The Hobbesian world that is poor, nasty, short and brutish, has been turned on its head. This new millennium, for most of the globe, ushers in a period that is comfortable, healthy, secure and long. Undoubtedly, this represents an extraordinary alteration in the human condition and an accomplishment of breathtaking proportions.

That said, it should also be noted that material advances are not a reflection of moral progress. As significant as technical innovation has been, it has not contributed to corresponding moral development. In fact, one might well conclude that there is an inverse relationship between material and moral progress.

Material progress has resulted in a rise of hedonism, family dissolution, the coarsening of culture and moral decay. Morality has in most aspects been outstripped by the preoccupation with material success and technical innovation.

There is, however, a person of rare insight who by dint of personal integrity and sheer will has broadened the public debate on American culture to include the moral dimensions of social policy. I am referring to John Howard, the author of the stirring words you are about to read.

Dr. Howard has been writing for decades on the current effect of the technical change on a society that has seemingly lost its moral moorings. He writes with passion, intelligence and common sense. And in my judgment he offers a pathway to recovery from the transgression of national memory loss.

Each essay in this book is a trail taking the reader through the thickets of history, until one appreciates the moral impulse that made this nation *sui generis*. To read Dr. Howard's book is to recall what Abraham Lincoln said about the national confusion during the Civil War: "When you are lost in life, do as you would if lost in a forest. Retrace your steps."

In glowing fashion, John Howard retraces those steps and, in the process, has produced an ennobling result.

CHAPTER I

INTRODUCTORY COMMENTARY

On April 20, 1999, Eric Harris and Dylan Kliebold carried out their plan to slaughter fellow students at Columbine High School in Colorado. It was an utterly horrifying crime. The American people were stunned. Clearly, action had to be taken to put a stop to the recurrent school ground shootings. The various efforts to accomplish that goal, reveal how little is understood about the Columbine tragedy. The provision of metal detectors, video monitors, increased security personnel and campaigns for more stringent gun control laws are all remedies directed at symptoms, only symptoms. The fundamental fact is that Eric Harris and Dylan Kliebold are savages, incapable of recognizing and refraining from an act of absolute evil. They are also the hapless victims of America's default in its primary obligation to its youth.

In all societies, each new generation must be trained how to live responsibly in it's own society. The social institutions, which normally perform this acculturation process, have become feeble tutors and education, which by definition should be most directly involved, has to a great extent, declared the acculturation of students to be taboo. The nation is now engulfed in the consequences of this ill-considered reversal—not only are there schoolboy gunmen, but also eminent national leaders devoid of morals and integrity; not only an entertainment industry striving to reach ever further toward the ultimate in shock, filth, degradation and scurrilous impiety, but also a public eager to consume its output; not only a populace increasingly fragmented into hostile groups, but also less and less able to find peace and fulfillment in their own lives.

The damage caused by repudiating Christendom's ideals, which used to be passed along from generation to generation, is not widely

13

understood. It is difficult for a person under the age of seventy to conceive of the American reality prior to World War II— the natural civility, the automatic trust in the strangers one encountered, and the preeminence of the family in one's daily life. The American spirit was unique, open, taken for granted and a source of pride. Life was more difficult then, before the great advances of medicine and technology, but for most people, even in the inner cities, life was pleasanter and more satisfying.

The analyses in this volume address various aspects of America's transformation from an amiable, civilized nation toward an aggressive, egocentric one. Written over almost four decades, this text reflects the mind-set of an educator whose studies in preparation for his career convinced him that a college president's foremost duty is to guide the development and refinement of the educational program. In a free nation, it is imperative that the students be helped to learn what it is to be responsible citizens, spouses, parents, neighbors, employees and children of God.

This concept of education was largely derived from doctoral studies that focused on the French historian, statesman and educational philosopher, Francois Guizot. He initiated and wrote a good part of the first French periodical devoted to educational matters. Subsequently, he drafted the legislation creating the first national system of elementary schools and was named Minister of Education to implement it. Twenty-five years later when the British government sent Matthew Arnold across the Channel to learn why the French educational system performed better than the British one, Arnold was told by almost everyone he encountered, that it was Guizot's concepts and continuing influence that accounted for the quality of French schooling.

In his educational periodical and on through six decades of public life, Guizot stressed that the fundamental purpose of education is the moral and ethical development of the students. "A sound body, a righteous mind and a virtuous character—these are what a good education must produce. This goal is invariable and universal." So began one of his first articles in his new magazine.

The study of Guizot's works led to the initiation in 1960 of an annual President's Opening Convocation to start each academic year at Rockford College with the President discussing some aspect of contemporary life he judged important for the students to ponder. Some of these chapters are analyses derived from those discourses. During the seventeen years at Rockford College and thereafter, speeches for other audiences and articles for various publications were written in the hope of providing understanding about difficulties or deterioration in various aspects of the American society, and about the principles which might be applied in alleviating them.

Any effort to bring principles to bear in modern decision-making will be in conflict with the tenor of the times. A principle is a prickly and unwelcome sort of thing nowadays because it is fixed and eternal and does not lend itself to bypassing or manipulating to meet individual desires. During the past century, change has come to be perceived as a virtue. In 1933, the city of Chicago celebrated its centennial with a world's fair devoted to the theme, "A Century of Progress." All forty-eight states, a great many foreign countries and most of the major industries provided a vast array of exhibits to dramatize the cultural and technological achievements of the human mind. The millions of visitors marveled at what they saw. It is unlikely that it occurred to any of them to question the validity of the theme. Man's progress was impressive and the world converged on Chicago to congratulate itself.

Since then the grand sweep toward an ever-brighter day has lost its momentum. Changes occur at a dizzying pace, but they include world hostilities and polarities, psychoses and neuroses, air and water pollution and a long list of other developments on the negative side of the ledger. Even so, the assumption that change equals progress persists. Corporations that used to emphasize their stability and venerability with reminders they had been in business since an ancient by-gone year, now work to give the impression of being ahead of the times. Even college admissions literature has undergone the same transition, with institutions all proclaiming themselves fertile sources of novelty, experiment and innovation.

Newness has come to be generally regarded as worthiness, although there is no rational basis for the equation. A devotion to change for the sake of change is just as simple-minded as a devotion to the status quo for the sake of status quo, but even more foolish. The status quo is at least the result of trial and error. In the May 1970 issue of the *Saturday Review*, Peter Schrag wrote, "To live or grow up in America in 1970 is to search for a center that doesn't exist... The events and forces we have created and which we honor, tend to displace and destroy...A generation ago, we regarded our discontinuities as signs of progress. Other things being equal, change was always for the better." After acknowledging that that faith in change was ill founded, he concludes, "We are now all refugees in our own country."

Throughout this volume it is assumed that many of the ideals and policies and standards of conduct which once prevailed in this nation were, in fact, more beneficial for the citizens and the society than the ones that supplanted them. It is also assumed the widespread prejudice against "turning back the clock," an aspect of the thoughtless allegiance to change, must not be permitted to block the restitution of solid time-tested principles that undergird a decent and godly civil order.

CHAPTER II

WORLD WAR II:
A HALF-CENTURY AND A WHOLE
CIVILIZATION AGO

5 December 1991
The Rockford (Illinois) Rotary Club

Japan's assault on Pearl Harbor was a thunderbolt that exploded in every living room in the United States. The battles and the bombing and the destruction in Europe which Americans had been watching from the balcony for two years were instantly no longer just somber news reports, but a terrible, frightening reality that had taken command of our lives.

For the men of draft age, the ultimate question of human existence was starkly catapulted to the top of the agenda. Are we merely clever animals that some improbable quirk of evolution has delivered, or are we children of God placed here with obligations to Him and to other human beings? Does the individual seek to save his own skin as his first and over-riding concern? Or are there ideals and linkages and duties that compellingly call him to serve his country's flag?

At that time and over the months that followed, many Americans volunteered for military duty, and millions were drafted with all but a small handful of them responding readily and serving creditably in the capacities to which they were assigned.

I was a member of a tank battalion in the First Infantry Division. Our unit participated in the D-Day landings in Normandy. Eleven months later, we met the Russians in Czechoslovakia as the

European part of the war came to an end. Most of those eleven months we were under enemy fire.

It is difficult for a person who hasn't experienced it to imagine what combat is like or to conceive of the emotional stress that accumulates. It is a shock to fire weapons at other human beings, and kill them; to adjust to a continuing series of deaths of people you have worked closely with and liked and counted on; to come to terms with the fear for your own life; to bear responsibility for life and death decisions some of which turn out badly for your comrades; to carry on through prolonged periods with next to no sleep; to spend day after day never knowing what will happen the next minute. After combat, the soldier is different from what he was before, emotionally scarred and to some extent estranged from family and friends. There is an intense and chaotic chapter of life that simply can't be shared. It is private and unspeakable.

The point of all this is not to drum up sympathy and applause fifty years after the fact. Rather, I want to focus on the performance of American's civilian military forces in that conflict. Despite relentless emotional stress only a very small percentage of the troops had psychological breakdowns, or combat fatigue as it was called, and not many turned to alcohol or drugs as an escape mechanism. The national psyche in that era was sturdy and resilient. And needed to be, not only for the pressures of fighting, but also for the ordeal of the training process.

Think for a minute about the raw material that became America's fighting troops. Our battalion was drafted from the state of Illinois. We had farm boys and factory workers, accountants and dishwashers, grocers and truck-drivers; we had a whole United Nations of Chicago ethnic groups; we had athletes and couch potatoes, we had people with graduate degrees and high school dropouts. It was the army's task to forge this hodge-podge of talents and attitudes into a physically fit, alert fighting force skilled in the use of complex weapons, battlefield tactics and other realms of mortally important knowledge.

Not only were the civilian recruits a mixed bag, but so were the people who trained them. The teachers were regular army sergeants and corporals. In order to provide sufficient instructional staff for the

18

avalanche of draftees, many army regulars were declared instant teachers although they were not suited for that work, by temperament, training or experience. The rapid transformation of millions of civilians into an effective fighting force was an amazing feat.

What were the features and conditions of the American reality fifty years ago that prepared the general populace to accept military service, to be undaunted by and profit from a crude training system, and to remain on an even keel emotionally through the rigors of warfare? There are, of course, no simple answers, but there are, I believe, some elements of the culture that had a powerful impact in shaping the character of the people of that time.

One was set forth in the book, *Man's Search for Meaning*, a narrative about one of Adolph Hitler's concentration camps. The author, Viktor Frankl, was an Austrian physician, incarcerated because he was a Jew. The prisoners were subjected to unbelievable extremes of cruelty, privation and persecution. They had inadequate clothing and housing and almost no food. They were forced to live in filth and were given no medical care. Dr. Frankl did what little he could for the sick and dying. Over a period of time, his physician's habit of observing the health of the people around him led to an astonishing discovery. The people who kept their strength and sanity the longest were not the ones who by brute strength or clever tricks obtained more than their share of the scarce food, but rather those who tried to be helpful to the other prisoners and shared with them what little they had. Their physical and mental condition seemed to be strengthened by their friendliness, their compassion, and their primary attentions devoted to something other than themselves.

At first, Dr. Frankl found this hard to believe, but as the months went by, his observation was thoroughly confirmed. It was clear to him that no matter how wretched and hopeless a situation may be, the individual has the freedom to choose how he will respond to that situation, and if the response is one of trying to make life better for others, that effort reinforces the individual's psychological and physical stamina. Most Americans of that era had already learned self-subordination and self-sacrifice.

Anyone who was old enough for military duty on December 7,

19

1941 had lived through the Great Depression. That phenomenon scarcely rates a footnote in today's history books, but it was, I assure you, a formative influence in the character of a generation of Americans. Consider, for example, the impact on the labor force. Jobs were scarce and people soon learned, if they didn't already know, that the employees who helped each other and did all they could to make the operation successful, had the best chance of keeping their jobs. If the boss was a grouch or didn't seem very bright, the worker still needed to do his best to find ways to get along with his employer. The folks who were always thinking about themselves, the quarrelsome ones and the chronic complainers soon discovered they weren't needed.

The financial bind of the depression had an impact on children, too. If they could obtain part-time work delivering newspapers or putting stock on the shelves of a store, or shining shoes, that income helped to put bread on the table. It also gave the children an early experience in the satisfaction of being helpful and they developed a valid sense of self-worth. With little money available for entertainment, and with no television, children read more than they do now. They played sandlot games of softball and touch football and learned how to get along with one another without the adult supervision of coaches and referees. The need to "make do" in the necessities of the household as well as in recreation was a good teacher of cooperation and interdependence.

Pre-World War II was also vastly different from today in the religious dimensions of American life. The importance of religion to emotional health was set forth by the Swiss psychiatrist Carl Jung in a book entitled *Psychotherapists or the Clergy*. He wrote:

> During the past thirty years, people from all the civilized countries of the earth have consulted me... There has not been one whose problem has not been finding a religious outlook on life. It is safe to say that every one of them fell ill because he had lost that which the living religions of every age have given to their followers, and none of them has been really healed who did not regain his religious outlook.

He was referring to the peace and stability that comes to the person who acknowledges a deity and a fixed set of ideals that provide a framework for living. America began as a religious nation and prior to World War II it was still widely assumed that people believed in God and belonged to a church or synagogue. The 'til death do us part in the marriage vows was still regarded as a commitment to God. Divorce was infrequent and those who did divorce were subject to both stigma and embarrassment. Blasphemy was not a subject for literature or for joking.

The respect for other people's religious commitments was such that no large private party or public event was held on Friday evening that did not provide a fish entree for the Roman Catholics in attendance, for in those days avoiding meat on that day was obligatory for them. The newspapers and magazines had no qualms about printing testimonies of religious faith. A particularly powerful one was printed as the editorial for *U.S. News and World Report* and was reprinted again several years later. It was written by Madame Chang Kai-shek in 1943, during the time she and her husband were trying to rally the Chinese people in territories already captured by the Communists. Here is an excerpt from her statement:

> Prayer is our source of guidance and balance. God is able to enlighten the understanding. I am often bewildered because my mind is only finite. I question and doubt my own judgments. Then I seek guidance and when I am sure, I go ahead, leaving the results with Him... I do not think it is possible to make this understandable to one who has not tried it. To explain to one who has no experience of getting guidance what it means would be like trying to make a stone-deaf person understand the beauty of a Chopin sonata.
>
> What I do want to make clear is that whether we get guidance or not, it is there. It is like tuning in on the radio. There's music in the air whether we tune in or not... With me religion is a very simple thing. It means to try with all my heart and soul and strength and mind to do the will of God.

It wasn't until 1947 that the United States Supreme Court

suddenly discovered that the First Amendment to the Constitution contained language that implied a wall of separation between church and state, although no such language appears in the text. Before that time biblical stories and biblical quotations and religious literature and prayers were an important and wholly expected element of American education in the public schools and colleges as well as the private ones. The impact of the banishment of God and faith and prayer from the educational process was manifest in national surveys conducted by the Princeton Religious Research Center founded by George Gallup.

A poll conducted in 1952, revealed that 64% of the 18-24 age group, whose schooling had taken place for the most part prior to the Supreme Court Decision, stated that religion was very important in their lives. Twenty-six years later only 37% of the same age group considered religion important in their lives. In 1958, 40% of the under-30 age group attended church weekly. Nineteen years later that figure had dropped to 29%. There was a 40% drop in both categories after the Supreme Court cleansed the schools of religion. Obviously, America's troops in World War II were the beneficiaries of the earlier kind of schooling.

Another dimension of the America of 50 years ago was the centrality of the family in the life of the people. We have already noted the children's role in helping to earn income in the depression and have indicated the infrequency of divorce. More needs to be said. Fourteen years ago our Rockford Institute sponsored the first national conference on the importance of the family and the need to reverse family disintegration. One of the speakers on that occasion talked about his own family, and said that although they had very little money, they had everything money can't buy. I have never read an essay that describes more accurately than that small phrase the blessings which a family can provide to its children. Most Americans going into military service in the 1940's carried with them the benefits of having lived in an intact family.

I want to conclude this rather subjective reflection on what America seemed to be in the 1940's with a quotation from one letter, the full text of another and a final comment. The first is a passage from the letter my mother tucked into my pocket as I went out the door to report for military service.

None of us knows what is in store for us in this life, but one thing is certain: if we live according to the noblest ideals of our faith and our traditions, we will have used well the time allotted to us. Faced with the prospect of combat, it may be tempting to set aside what we know is right. A high price is paid for such a departure. Others *may* suffer for our lapses; we *always* do. It is an earned privilege to hold your head high.

The other letter is from Jacob L. Devers, the Commanding General of the United States Army. It is dated December 18, 1945.

Dear Lieutenant Howard:

Your recent return to the civilian pursuits which you left at our country's call, prompts me to express my sincere appreciation for the service you have rendered the Army Ground Forces.

Our victory would not have been possible without your aid and the aid of other citizens who, like you, left their homes and families to defend our principles of freedom.

The responsibilities of members of a citizen army have not ceased with the termination of hostilities. I know that you realize your duties to your Government as a private citizen all the more as a result of your military experience.

I know too, that you will always remember, with pleasure and just pride, the friendships you have made, your experiences with the finest Army in the world and the sincere gratitude of our Nation.

That letter, too, represents the civilization that once prevailed in this land, speaking openly and proudly of the responsibilities of the citizens. The remarkable performance of America's military forces in that era was, I am firmly convinced, a reflection of the then reigning culture, in which responsibilities to God, to country, to community, to neighbors and to family were willingly accepted as the givens of life in America.

23

CHAPTER III

THE FLOUNDERING FREE SOCIETY OR WISDOM VANQUISHED BY EXPERTISE

March 21, 1983
Chief Executives Forum at Scottsdale, Arizona

Once, after I had finished a talk for the Young President's Organization, the next speaker, America's all-purpose genius, Buckminster Fuller, mounted the rostrum. He said that before he turned to his prepared remarks, he wanted to say something to that fellow who just finished. "You folks in the colleges," he said, glaring at me, "are going to be the ruination of the country. What you do is to identify the bright students as they come through and make them experts in something. That has some usefulness, but the trouble is that it leaves the ones with mediocre intelligence and the dunderheads to become the generalists who must serve as the college presidents." When the laughter subsided, he added, " And Presidents of the United States."

As usual, Fuller had put his finger on something basic. He was altogether right, but that little bombshell of wisdom that he dropped isn't restricted to those two showcase vocations. Every time a policy decision is made which affects a large segment of the population, the decision-makers ought to have the advice of generalists with a broad knowledge of history and philosophy, counselors who understand human nature, who understand the interdependence of the various basic institutions of the society and their vulnerability. In brief, the decision-makers need the help of people who have some realistic chance of accurately forecasting the long-range consequences of their decisions.

When you think about the far-reaching dimensions of Mr. Fuller's insight, you sense this may be a reason why nothing seems to work right any more. Perhaps we are so impressed with expertise and so disinclined to seek out wisdom that we have brought upon ourselves many of the social, economic, political and psychological difficulties that beset us today.

In order to understand and reverse the disintegration of all those social systems which once made it possible for people to live and work together amicably and productively, it will be necessary to rediscover the principles that make those systems operable. All of us readily understand that if we redesign an airplane in defiance of the principles of aerodynamics, that plane isn't going to fly. We seem to have forgotten, however, that there are principles just as rigid and inevitable that apply to free institutions— the economy, the government, the laws, the schools, the press, the criminal justice system—and we have been changing these systems and assigning new functions to them on the advice of experts, with unintentional but damaging disregard for the overall governing principles of society.

Let's turn to one of the astonishing minds of Western civilization, whose passion was to identify principles, in order to view some of the troubling and mystifying questions we face, through the lenses of clarity that he provided. Our guide is the Baron Charles de Montesquieu. In 1748, he published his magnum opus, *The Spirit of the Laws*. Many scholars regard it as the most important work of political philosophy since the intellectual giants of classical times. His analyses were well known to, and heavily drawn upon by the remarkable men who fashioned the American Constitution four decades after his book was published.

Montesquieu observed that each form of government has a particular relationship with its citizens and that when that relationship changes, the form of government is in trouble. In the case of a despotism or dictatorship, the requirement is a constant state of fear on the part of the people. When the people are no longer afraid of their rulers, dictatorship is in trouble. We have seen the draconian measures used by the Soviet Union to strike terror into the hearts of the peoples of the satellite nations. Poland is a particular threat to Russia's authoritarian regime, because large numbers of the citizens are willing to risk imprisonment or death to be relieved of the Communist oppression. The mounting reports of the Soviet mass slaughter of women and children in Afghanistan villages reflect one technique by which despotism can frighten people into submission.

A monarchy, Montesquieu noted in comparison, has as its indispensable requirement loyalty on the part of the people. When that loyalty wavers, the monarchy crumbles.

A republic which elects its officers, Montesquieu said, is the most desirable form of government but also the most difficult to sustain, for its existence requires a virtuous populace. When the people are no longer virtuous, he explained, the republic falters.

Why is that? Why is virtue a necessity in a free society and not in other forms of government?

Every one of us is subject to a continuing tension between what we might like to do at a given moment and what we are supposed to do as a member of any group. This tension applies to all of our associations- the family, the church, the bridge club, the athletic team, the kindergarten, or the nation. Each group has to have some way to ensure the cooperation of the participants so that the purposes of the group can be fulfilled. You cannot have your employees pouring Coca Cola on the computer or singing "The Pilgrim's Chorus" in the vice- president's office whenever it suits their fancy. You cannot have the pitcher tackling a runner on the way to first, in order to give a clumsy shortstop more time for his throw. You cannot have the child putting down the stopper in the washbasin and letting the faucets run. That's a no-no. A non-negotiable no-no. It makes no difference how much he likes to see the water running down the hall.

So, too, with a nation. There has to be some way to bring about the cooperation of the citizens in order that the common interests may be served. As Montesquieu noted, the dictatorship enforces its rule by harsh techniques, which now include terrorism, secret police, psychiatric imprisonment, brainwashing, propaganda, and other methods that keep the citizens fearful and docile. At the opposite end of the governmental spectrum is what is called a free society. Note that phrase "what is called." A free society is not one in which everybody does his own thing. That wouldn't be any society at all but a jungle populated with savages. The accurate definition of a savage is a person who does his own thing, without regard to anyone else. In the free society, the characteristic means for achieving cooperation is the voluntary observance, not of laws, but of informal codes of conduct. These codes are innumerable and include religious commandments, professional ethics, the house rules of every organization, sportsmanship, manners, morals, patriotism, loyalty, lawfulness, fidelity, truthfulness, integrity, respect for one's neighbor, giving a good day's work for a good day's pay, and many others. This is simply an elaboration of Montesquieu's comprehensive term virtue.

When these informal codes of conduct break down and large numbers of citizens revert to the savage inclinations to rob, steal, cheat, vandalize, and disregard the rights of others, then the citizens call upon the government to pass more and more laws, regulating the details of citizen behavior. New legions of inspectors, compliance officers, and police must be mobilized, and the society in question moves along the spectrum from freedom toward the centrally regulated despotism. And that, friends, is what has been happening at an accelerating pace in the United States.

History makes it abundantly clear that there is nothing in the human genetic system that inclines the person to behave in a civilized fashion. The haunting ballad from *South Pacific* which says you have to be taught to hate and fear is a lovely sentiment but it has got the thing exactly wrong. On the contrary, you have to be taught to respect, cooperate with, and love your neighbor. This process of socialization is the most fundamental requirement for sustaining a free society and it is one that has dwindled away in the United States. American education performed this function intentionally and quite effectively for about 150 years. But education has withdrawn from this role, and to a great extent now prides itself on not teaching any particular values to the students. The new academic orthodoxy proclaims all points of view to be equally welcome.

Let us now direct the Montesquieu lens toward capitalism. A year ago I was in Europe as an American delegate to an international conference on the future of nuclear energy. My topic was the antinuclear activism in the United States. Because my position was essentially sympathetic to industry, I was asked if I would be willing to lecture on the subject of capitalism at a nearby German university. The class to which I spoke was a graduate seminar in English language and culture. By the time the class began, the room was filled to overflowing. The seminar leader said to me with some consternation that the posted announcement seemed to have drawn every leftist activist in the vicinity. I began my talk and immediately there was an undercurrent of grumbling and conversation, so I stopped and said, "There seem to be people here who would rather talk than listen, so let's hear about it." The pre-selected spokesman stood up and said, "It is unthinkable to us that anyone who has been the head of an American academic institution would have anything good to say about capitalism. It is a system designed to make the rich and powerful richer and more powerful. It is only because of government intervention that the workers get a decent wage and have proper working conditions. Without government pressures, capitalists gouge the customers with shoddy and dangerous products, and act in collusion to fix prices. American capitalism cares nothing for the poor, the sick, and the hungry in either its own country or the less fortunate nations, except to try to bleed them for profits." This indictment drew extended applause.

The question arises: How do you respond to that view of our economic system? Many, perhaps most, of the spokesmen for capitalism would point to the track record of the market economy: its historical success in delivering goods and services far better than any other economic system and in raising the population's standard of living as well. That line of reasoning is persuasive and sufficient for the business executive. However, it doesn't begin to penetrate the animosity of the convinced anti-capitalist, who will usually respond by saying, "There you go again. You and your standard of living. All you care about is money. We care about people."

Of much greater importance, this response leaves unanswered the dynamite criticism that capitalism, and especially the profit motive, drives people to trample on other people in order to increase the bottom line. This allegation must be dealt with, for it lies at the heart

29

of the ideological struggle in which the world is involved. Although this is an altogether erroneous allegation, it has been repeated so often and so insistently that it has come to be regarded as an article of revealed truth. Is it false because these problems don't occur in our places of business? No, they occur with distressing frequency in our business community and among doctors, teachers, social workers, journalists, and members of every other profession. Instead, it is untrue because the profit motive is not the cause of cruel, deceitful and dishonest behavior. There is nothing inherent in the private-enterprise system that impels people to behave irresponsibly.

The miracle of American capitalism advanced hand in hand with the most prodigious outpouring of individual, group, and national generosity the world has ever witnessed. When Alexis de Tocqueville took the pulse of American reality in the mid- 19th century, he concluded that public- spiritedness was one of the primary characteristics of the American nation. He wrote about the readiness of citizens to band together to assist people who needed help or to improve some public condition. These were voluntary, pervasive, responsible, and effective initiatives of a populace operating within a private- enterprise economy. Virtue still prevailed in the business community, as elsewhere in America in the 19th century.

The fact is that dishonesty, disregard for one's neighbors and selfishness are all aspects of individual character. If large numbers of people behave callously or deceitfully, that reflects a failure of the schools, the churches, the families, the literature, and all the other cultural institutions that have the function of shaping the character of the people. It is one of the tragic ironies of our era that the capitalistic system has been tagged with the blame for irresponsible and destructive behavior, when that blame rightfully falls on the very people who are pointing the finger at capitalism- the clergy, the professors, the authors, and the social commentators. Theirs is the responsibility to transmit ideals and standards, to build a responsible populace. This is one of the large principles of the free society that we have forgotten. And it is one that needs to be forcefully and persistently reintroduced into the marketplace of ideas throughout the world.

There is one passage in Montesquieu that deserves special study and contemplation in this period when the nuclear freeze occupies such a prominent place on the agenda. The quotation is taken from the second chapter of Book Four of *The Spirit of the Laws*. It occurs under the subheading, "That Honor is not the Principle of Despotic Government":

> ...As honor has its laws and rules... it can be found only in countries in which the constitution is fixed, and where (the nations) are governed by settled laws...
>
> Honor (is) a thing unknown in arbitrary governments, some of which have not even a proper word to express it.

The latter phrase should haunt us, for when a Western nation negotiates a treaty, the supposition is that both sides will yield some concessions and arrive at a compromise. The Western nation then expects to honor that treaty. But what about the despotism, where "honor" has no meaning?

Well, this has been an exercise in the kind of broad-gauged analysis that Buckminster Fuller said was being phased out of modern deliberations and judgments.

As we all know in our businesses and in our families, if we can get our thinking straight, if we can penetrate to the core of the problems we face, that is the most important step on the way to a brighter day.

Finally, let us take courage from the concluding passage of de Tocqueville's *Democracy in America*:

> I am aware that many of my contemporaries think that nations on earth are never their own masters and that they are bound to obey some insuperable and unthinking power, the product of pre-existing facts, of race, or soil, or climate.
>
> These are false and cowardly doctrines which can only produce feeble men and pusillanimous nations. Providence did not make mankind entirely free or completely enslaved. Providence has, in truth, drawn a predestined circle around each man beyond which he cannot pass; but within those vast limits

man is strong and free, and so are peoples.

The nations of our day cannot prevent conditions of equality from spreading in their midst. But it depends upon themselves whether equality is to lead to servitude or freedom, knowledge or barbarism, prosperity or wretchedness.

That balance which de Tocqueville poses will be tipped according to whether wisdom or expertise shall prevail.

CHAPTER IV

HOW DID WE GET INTO THIS MESS?

Keynote Address by
Dr. John A. Howard –
Director, Rockford College Institute
at Annual state convention
Arkansas Farm Bureau Federation
Little Rock, Arkansas
November 30, 1978

I am honored to take part in your program, because the Farm Bureau is one organization that tackles problems head-on, standing proudly for the principles of reverence for God, hard work, honesty, individual responsibility, and the abiding importance of the traditional family as the fundamental unit of American society. Those are the principles that made this nation strong and good, and those are the principles that can make it strong again. But some rather foolish people, with loud voices, have been promoting an altogether different set of principles and because those new principles seemed attractive and didn't seem to involve any hard work or sacrifice, the new principles have come to dominate our society and now we have trouble on all sides.

At the time the United States became a nation, the justifying principle was liberty. It was the hope of freedom from unjust taxes and tyrannous government that caused the troops to fight the long arduous Revolutionary War, and the protection of liberty was, of course, the explicit purpose of the Bill of Rights. As long as the preservation of liberty remained the top priority of the American Government, the nation continued to grow stronger subject, of course, to the ups and downs which affect all human affairs. As long as the protection of liberty remained the top priority of the national government, the people of the country were able to live in reasonable harmony with each other except for the Civil War, which was, in fact, a disagreement about the nature of liberty and the individuals to whom the privileges of liberty should be available. For a century and a half, the folks in Washington, for the most part, saw their primary role as assisting, supporting and protecting the proper activities of the citizens as they carried out the purposes of their own lives, the government mediating their conflicts and protecting their persons from assault and their property from theft and vandalism and the nation from foreign aggression.

Then in the middle third of this century, there was a second American Revolution, which radically changed the nature of our government and created a different relationship between the government and the people. The American Government of today operates on new assumptions and is structured to serve new purposes with the result that liberty, as it was understood two hundred years ago, is no longer a major concern of the government. Because we didn't see any barricades in the streets or any bleeding casualties in this Second American Revolution, many citizens suppose that we still have the same government that was founded by our forefathers, although one that has been adapted to meet what we have been told are the needs of the twentieth century. If people do believe it is still the same government, they are greatly mistaken. The protection of liberty has been replaced by the granting of privileges, benefits and services. That is the new justifying principle, not liberty, but the distribution of gifts and favors. Even our foreign policy now seems to be determined by which pressure groups the government has decided to please.

This change of governmental purpose was welcomed by many citizens. The hardships imposed by the Great Depression seemed to be sufficient reason to use the vast powers and funds of the Washington government to assist people in their time of need. The openhearted citizens eventually became accustomed to having the

Congress authorize help for an endless list of folks who asked for help. Unfortunately, the voters who supported this change in the activities of the government did not understand nor anticipate what happens to a government when it gets into the business of giving; the citizens did not foresee the devastating interplay between the power of those in office to grant favors and the eagerness of the citizens to receive favors.

The *dream* of a kinder and more humane society has turned into a *nightmare* of governmental extravagance and corruption, of unfulfilled promises on a gigantic scale, of ill-conceived, often counterproductive and unnecessarily costly programs, and a populace increasingly divided into militant groups competing fiercely against each other for the favors given out by the government. We are steadily moving into the proverbial war of all against all, with everyone trying to get special privileges for himself or his group.

The disastrous consequences of the welfare state government as opposed to the government of liberty are apparent on all sides, but let us examine several of those consequences, which have twisted and distorted specific aspects of our government and ruined its relationships with the people.

1. The Congress, as you know, has the job of thinking through and then passing the laws that govern all the citizens of the nation. Since those laws apply to everyone, it is fitting they should be discussed and voted upon by delegates elected from across the country. If bad laws are enacted, each citizen has his own Congressmen and Senators whom he can hold accountable for the vote, and whom he can call upon to seek to have the law changed if it was a bad law that unjustly injures him.

However, once the Congress opened the floodgates to the great ocean of laws providing special privileges for special groups, it became utterly impossible for our elected representatives to give proper attention to the enormous volume of legislation proposed and passed. It is tragic and irresponsible that the legislators are voting into law many bills, which they do not fully understand, the results of which they do not begin to foresee, but an even more disturbing problem has arisen. In some instances, the actual lawmaking function has simply been passed on to non-elected bureaucrats in other parts of the government. The Congress has made lawmakers out of minor functionaries who aren't even known to the voters. In a speech before a group of college presidents, the Director of the Office of Civil Rights in the Department of Health, Education and Welfare reported on several major civil rights laws which had been phrased only in general terms by the Congress, leaving the actual provisions of the law to be written by the staff of his Civil Rights office. The Constitution of the United States was not designed to serve a welfare state, and the Congress, now hopelessly snowed under by the welfare state activities it has generated, is evading, at least in part, its primary Constitutional function.

2. The change from the protection of liberty to the giving of benefits and privileges has also fundamentally twisted the basis on which the voters judge who is the best candidate for national office. To an increasing extent, honesty, extensive knowledge, good judgment and the other sound and honorable qualities which one would hope to find in candidates for high office are being cast aside in favor of a very different set of characteristics. In the new order, when voters are concerned about what benefits the elected officer will provide for them, promises, hypocrisy, deceit, log-rolling leverage and clout are fast becoming the characteristics of electability. As Harold Blake Walker noted, of twenty-one Congressmen linked in one way or another with political wrongdoing or personal scandal prior to the 1976 election, nineteen were re-elected. Criminal activity and flagrant immorality have become insignificant in the minds of the greedy voters of the welfare state. Even those legislators who take pride in their integrity and moral righteousness are sometimes those who try the hardest to convince the voters that they can provide more benefits to their district than can the opponent, crassly appealing to the greed of the people who cast the ballots. The welfare state has made honesty and principles unnecessary attributes of the office seeker.

3. Another massive and destructive consequence of the Second Revolution is the change in the purpose of taxation. When liberty was the by-word, taxes were collected only to pay to operate the government. Now a large and rapidly growing portion of the taxes

is collected for the express purpose of redistributing the wealth. This concept denies the meaning of private property. Once redistribution is accepted as a proper function of government there is, of course, no logical point at which to stop until you have achieved the total equalization of whatever wealth still exists. And there won't be much then. The confiscation of assets discourages productive people from working hard, and encourages lazy people to loaf. The redistribution of wealth by the government is the kiss of death to an economy and it is necessarily and eternally the enemy of liberty.

4. The new role of government also brings into sharp focus a wasteful self-contradiction of bureaucracy. If people are employed to attend to a problem, the last thing they want to do is solve that problem and put themselves out of work. One can only regard with awe and admiration the great skill of the bureaucrats in magnifying a problem into something of gigantic proportions, generating research, undertaking surveys, holding conferences, traveling to the far corners of the earth to learn if the residents of Oz and Shangri-La have the same problem, preparing reports, holding press conferences, appointing committees, expanding the staff, opening regional offices, hiring consultants, publishing articles, visiting campuses, etc., all intently focused upon the problem usually without any measurable effect in reducing it. As an example, consider the matter of illegal mind-altering drugs. Before the government problem-solvers got into the act, a number of private service organizations were trying to deal with this troublesome difficulty, operating with a relatively modest amount of money. Once Washington spread its welfare state arms to embrace this grand problem, a new industry, the anti-drug abuse industry, blossomed into a billion-dollars-a-year enterprise virtually overnight. There is no data to indicate that drug problems have diminished as a result of this massive spending activity. Indeed, the use of cocaine has been swiftly increasing, and there are believable reports that even the staff of the White House is involved in the use of illegal drugs. The bureaucracy has a fairly consistent record of not solving the problems it tackles, thus assuring that the jobs of the problem-solvers will be safeguarded and multiplied.

Well, these four points—the partial transfer of the lawmaking function by the Congress to bureaucrats in the legislative branch, the acceptance by the voters of dishonesty and blatant immorality in candidates for high office if they can just deliver enough favors to their constituents, the collection of taxes for the express purpose of redistributing the wealth, and the inescapable contradiction of the bureaucrats' not wanting to put themselves out of work by solving the problems they were hired to work on,—these constitute just a sampling of the damage that has come from the revolutionary change in the justifying principle of our government.

In a book entitled *The End of the American Era*, the author, Andrew Hacker, has made a dire prediction:

> Only a few decades remain to complete the era America will have known as a nation. For the United States has embarked on its decline since the closing days of the Second World War...It is too late in our history to restore order or reestablish authority: the American temperament has passed the point where self-interest can subordinate itself to citizenship.

Mr. Hacker has brutally identified the basic question: Have the American people reached the point were they are so bent on gratifying their passions without restraint and so determined to have the government solve all their problems that they are no longer capable of restoring the basic principles of liberty, of reasserting the reverence for God, personal integrity, lawfulness, a commitment to the sanctity of the family, economic self-reliance, patriotism and a decent regard for one's neighbor?

Well, friends, I think Mr. Hacker is wrong. I believe this whole thing can be turned around. One of the reasons I think so is this assembly right here and its counterparts in all the other states. The American Farm Bureau Federation has woven those principles into the whole range of its policies for 1978. And there is a growing number of organizations that are also committed to reestablishing those principles: The General Federation of Women's Clubs, the American Mothers Committee, Morality In Media, the National Federation of Decency, an increasing number of columnists and corporations, the Eagle Forum, the whole hierarchy of the Mormon

Church and many others.

To conclude, we need to remember that the important things in this world are never easy. The Good Lord didn't design it that way. If we have big problems, that's all right. We just have to try to understand them and then roll up our sleeves and get to work. I hope that what I have said may be helpful in understanding the problems that confront us so that we can re-earn a decent and a responsible society, which is the proud heritage of America.

CHAPTER V

LEGALIZED GAMBLING – A FOOLISH BET

Persuasion At Work Newsletter
September 1979

For centuries, foolish but determined people labored to convert base metals into gold. This prolonged effort was a monumental fiasco. The latter-day counterpart of this medieval quest for the free lunch is the effort to replenish a hard-pressed public treasury with revenues derived from the extension of legalized gambling, including and especially the establishment of state lotteries. But there is a difference, and a critically important one. Whereas the alchemist wasted only his own time and resources, the current thrust for easy public wealth lays waste to the framework of an ordered and productive society in a manner that is progressively more difficult to repair.

Before examining the specific damage, let us recognize that the business community plays an influential, albeit unintended, role in this surging phenomenon. According to accounts in various business journals, gambling has become one of the most promising "growth industries." It is now discussed on the financial pages in the same tone of voice as might be used to report on the remarkable success of a breakthrough in solar heat or a quick cure for the common cold. The treatment of gambling-related securities as just another investment opportunity contributes directly to the desensitization of public attitudes toward an activity that has, historically, flashed a warning signal to many. Just as the "wrongness" of breaking the law has been dissipated by the uncritical public acceptance of marijuana use, so the "wrongness" of governmentally endorsed gambling is being eroded by the classification of this activity as just another commercial enterprise.

What's the Problem?

Well, what is the harm of putting an official seal of approval on and deriving some revenues from an activity that has flourished throughout history? The quick answer is, what is the harm of legitimizing theft, which also has an ancient tradition? Ah, but this one doesn't damage anyone else. Wrong! Wrong on six counts!

1. Any civilization is only made possible as techniques are developed which will effectively restrain certain human tendencies. One of these tendencies is the effort to get something for nothing, or in its milder form, to try to get something for less than its value. Theft, embezzlement, bribery, blackmail, hijacking, robbery, looting and many other kinds of plunder are manifestations of this natural inclination. America's best hope for salvaging a viable private enterprise system from the accelerating progression into the spendthrift welfare state is to diminish the popular belief that government can provide a free lunch. The State of Illinois is now celebrating the fifth year of its lottery and the airwaves and billboards are cluttered with ingenious invitations to try one's luck for the quick buck. Chicago's mayor has just proposed a casino "equal to anything in Monte Carlo"[1] as a financial shot in the arm for the city's insufficient revenues. This systematic encouragement for the public to seek something for nothing is folly compounded. The successful free society is dependent upon a citizenry convinced that it must earn its way, and the government, above all, should help to develop this conviction.

2. "Gambling is the principal source of income for organized criminal gangs in the country,"[2] reported the Kefauver Crime

---

[1] *Chicago Tribune,* Sept. 12, 1979, p. 1.

[2] President's Commission on Law Enforcement and Administration of Justice, *Task Force Report: Organized Crime* (Washington, 1967), p. 2. footnote 20.

Committee in 1951; in 1962 the Senate's Committee on Government Operations confirmed that "organized crime is primarily dependent upon illicit gambling, a multi-billion dollar market, for the necessary funds required to operate other criminal and illegal activities or enterprises."[3] While exact figures are, of course, impossible to determine, professional estimates of the total amount wagered in all forms of "nonsocial" gambling in America range from $75 to $500 billion a year; of this total, eighty to ninety percent is thought to be illegal. Organized criminal activity accounts for the vast majority of this illegal gambling action, from which profits flow to finance its other activities, such as prostitution, drugs, labor racketeering and graft. Gambling revenue is the life-blood of the most pernicious element in our society.

3. Legal gambling provides another productive field for criminal activity. Organized crime thrives on revenues from its *illegal* gambling operations, but also exploits the opportunities that *legalized* gambling offers. Legal casinos, like those in Las Vegas and Atlantic City, provide fertile territory for aggressive organized criminal infiltration. "It is now clear that organized crime has been planning an Atlantic City take-over for at least the past seven years," writes Michael Dorman in *New York* magazine. The mob was also "instrumental in pushing through the very legislation signed by [Governor Brendan] Byrne, and already has a tight grip on both the casino front and gambling's lucrative sidelines."[4] New Jersey's Attorney General was well aware of this when, after a year-long investigation, he recommended against granting a permanent license to the only casino that had opened so far, on the basis of evidence, which pointed to extensive involvement of organized crime in the operation. And one of the five commissioners who had to approve the license said he did so only with great reservations: "There was a tremendous desire to get the first casino open willy-nilly"[5] —a

---

[3] *Ibid.,* p. 2, footnote 20.

[4] *New York Magazine*, Jan, 30, 1979, p. 40.

[5] *Parade*, June 10, 1979, p. 9.

sentiment shared by other states and municipalities eager to cash in on the "easy money." Public officials looking for the quick-fix of gambling revenue should study the report on gambling in the *Wall Street Journal* which relates "how the underworld slices away millions of dollars before the very eyes of suspicious state [gambling] regulators" in Nevada (September 10, 1979, p. 1). The *New York Times Magazine* reports

the legalization of casino gambling has transformed Atlantic City into a new frontier for organized crime.... members and associates of at least four organized crime groups are trying to capitalize on the casino gambling boom.[6]

4. Legalized gambling generates new clientele for the mob's gambling operations since the gambler soon discovers that the odds from legal betting are not as good as those in illegal operations in which neither the operator nor the bettor pays taxes. As the Commission on the Review of the National Policy Towards Gambling said in 1967:

It is axiomatic that the two principal goals of legalized gambling—revenue raising and crime control—are incompatible. The taxation and other tribute necessary to generate significant profits for government may place the legal entrepreneur at an impossible competitive disadvantage with his illegal counterpart, who is not so burdened. If government is seriously to challenge the role of illegal gambling—particularly that part of it controlled by organized crime—then the legal entity may have to offer competitive odds and payoffs. It may also have to eliminate taxes on the bettor and the operator—which would, of necessity, eliminate the likelihood of substantial government revenue.[7]

---

[6] *New York Times Magazine*, Feb. 5, 1979, p. 10.

[7] Commission on the Review of the National Policy Toward Gambling, *Gambling in America*

5. The law enforcement system is compromised. A 1978 study of gambling law enforcement in major American cities showed that officers of the law sensed little public support for enforcing the gambling laws. "In general, officers felt that increased legalization made gambling enforcement more frustrating...Furthermore, the discontent and frustration combined with the lack of support from others might well contribute to a climate conducive to corruption."[8]

Rufus King, who served as attorney for Senator Kefauver's Crime Committee in the 1950's, with Attorney General Robert F. Kennedy through 1963, and who prepared the report on gambling for the President's Organized Crime Task Force in 1967, made the strongest possible case against legalized gambling:

The legalization of professional gambling should not be endorsed or encouraged in any form or at any level. *Licensed gambling activities simply cannot be effectively controlled by public authorities in a democratic society; sooner or later, they're always corrupt.*[9] [Emphasis in original]

King estimated that approximately 30% of the profits of organized crime's gambling enterprises "finds it's way directly and indirectly into the hands of corrupt public officials and law enforcers."[10]

It is folly for government to take actions which promote new

(Washington, 1976), p. 1.

[8] Floyd J. Fowler, et al., *Gambling Law Enforcement in Major American Cities* (Washington, 1978), pp. 104, 114.

[9] Rufus King, *Gambling and Organized Crime* (Washington, 1969), pp. 168-9.

[10] *Ibid.*, p. 10.

levels of bribery when law enforcement officers are already crippled by the curtailment of intelligence gathering and by the evidentiary proceedings imposed by the courts in the past 15 years.

6. The surge of gambling contaminates other institutions. Today's media promote illegal gambling functions, regularly featuring famous Las Vegas bookmakers on television before game time and even advising listeners how they might find a local illegal bookmaker.[11] The integrity of college athletic events has been so imperiled by the pressure of bettors intent on "making the spread" that the Collegiate Sports Information Directors Association has formed a permanent Gambling Awareness Committee to bring these problems to the attention of the public.[12] Their efforts have received enthusiastic support from coaches' associations and the NCAA's Committee to Combat Legalized Gambling. Clearly, college authorities now recognize the danger for the athletic programs with the likelihood of "fixed" games increasing as gambling becomes more "respectable," and integrity less so.

The alchemists in the political profession who promise a free lunch to the citizens in their own lives or who promise it to the city, state or nation in which they hold formal responsibilities are either naive or unscrupulous. It has been observed that societies seldom choose the right answers to the big problems until they have exhausted all the wrong answers, which seem to be available at a smaller cost. The use of legalized gambling as a source of public revenue is unmistakably a wrong answer. The actual cost is far too high.

[11] Tom Brokaw and Pete Axtelheim, *Today,* Sept. 7, 1979.

[12] *CoSIDA Report*, March 1978, pp. 10-11; *Sporting News,* Feb. 25, 1978.

CHAPTER VI

A SURE COMPASS: AMERICAN SOCIETY HAS LOST ITS SENSE OF DIRECTION

By John A. Howard, Counselor,
The Rockford Institute
Delivered at the 25th Anniversary of *St. Croix Review*, St. Paul, Minnesota, October 21, 1992

But what more oft in nations grown corrupt
And by their vices brought to servitude
Than to love bondage more than liberty,
Bondage with ease than strenuous liberty.
John Milton, *Samson Agonistes* (1671)

We have gathered to celebrate the founding of a modest journal by an Australian clergyman a quarter of a century ago. And we come to give thanks for the wisdom he has consistently disseminated. Wisdom is always a scarce commodity, but in this age when the worship of the individual has virtually abolished the conventions of civilized living, the wisdom presented in the *St. Croix Review* has been a godsend to readers who yearn for a revival of decent, moral and lawful communities.

Decency, morality and lawfulness were still commonly accepted patterns for living in 1967 when Angus McDonald began his magazine. Those virtues were woven into the culture. They described behavior that was simply expected of people. Their importance and their benefits were taken for granted. The value of standards which embody obligations to the community cannot be overstated. What people believe, what they cherish, what they will sacrifice for, what they regard as trivial—these are the influences which shape the destiny of a family, a business firm, a community or a nation.

Now, however, decency, lawfulness, morality and many other ancient proprieties have been stripped of their authority. They have been supplanted by different views, which glorify personal preferences with no consideration for the well-being, or even the survival, of the group. Just how different the new attitudes are was made clear in a recent interview with Michael Blonsky, an analyst of cultural trends. He is a professor at New York University. The interview took place at Nike Town, a glittering new store on Chicago's Michigan Avenue that sells wildly-expensive sneakers. "This," said Blonsky on entering the store, "is a church! A post-modern church!" Then pointing to a life-sized figure of Michael Jordan, the basketball star, he declared, "Look! There's God!"

This was not just crude and blasphemous flippancy. He went on to explain that many people today are totally unpersuaded by any system of beliefs. For them flashy shoes are as important as anything gets. Beyond a fascination with the ownership of impressive things, Blonsky cites as other key values of the New Culture glamour, fitness, youth, power, freedom, eroticism and violence.

"In the 1960s and 1970s," Blonsky noted, "The human psyche began to be reordered, it got altered. The feeling is people are being produced that are different from before World War II."

Well, I must admit the professor is on to something there. Something big! For anyone who was an adult before World War II, it is hard to believe the populace he is describing is from the same country as the Americans of pre-World War II vintage. Or even the same species. Violence and sneakers are some of the most important things in life? One is inclined to wonder what strange thing has happened to younger generations, deadening their souls and afflicting their minds with foolish notions.

How did this transformation of America's beliefs come about? How was it possible so broadly and so quickly to discredit and displace the ancient settled concepts, which for generations had guided and knitted together the common life? One solid account of that change is set forth by Todd Gitlin in a book entitled *The Sixties, Years of Hope, Days of Rage.* Gitlin's bright mind surfaced early. He was valedictorian of his class at The Bronx High School of Science. He went on to Harvard University and in 1963, he was elected national president of the Students for a Democratic Society, or SDS as it was commonly known. That was the brain-trust of the revolutionary groups of the Sixties. Gitlin was in the thick of the protests and confrontations all across the country, including the shocking turmoil at the 1968 Democratic Convention in Chicago. He visited Castro's Cuba. His book is an effort to distill the significance of that decade of turbulence.

In the summary I offer here of the repudiation by young Americans of the established order, I am much indebted to Gitlin's analysis. First, the context. During the 1950's, America was prosperous. It was the one powerful, respected nation of the world. By and large, the population was comfortable, happy and confident about the future. Things were going well for the United States. Even so, the children growing up in that period became increasingly uneasy about the possibility of atomic warfare. There were bomb shelters and school evacuation drills and there was much public distress about the Soviet Union's spreading its Marxist doctrines across the globe. The East West tensions took on the ominous title of the Cold War.

Another cause of distress was America's failure to give a fair shake to its Black citizens, brought into sharp focus by the Civil Rights Movement and the cruel efforts to suppress it. In households like the Gitlins' where the liberal parents had regularly voiced their sympathy for down-trodden peoples throughout the world, it was a natural thing for the children to rejoice when the repressive Batista regime of Cuba was overthrown by Fidel Castro and his band of revolutionaries. The humanitarian claims of socialism seemed a welcome contrast to the American reality.

In addition to being troubled by the Bomb and America's unfair treatment of the Blacks, the baby boom generation became increasingly worried as the Vietnam conflict expanded and the draft took a growing portion of the young men. Allegations that America was fighting an unjust war for the benefit of special interests were perhaps too readily accepted, without much thought about whether they were true. When it turned out that the "good guys" who had freed the Cuban people from oppression were, in fact, Communists, that revelation, for many who were nervous about The Bomb, raised doubts about whether America should even be trying to contain Communism. Maybe America's anti-Communist foreign policy was a bad idea rather than a good one.

Further inciting the growing antagonism toward the government was the discrepancy between the 18-year-old draft age and the 21-year-old voting age. This was a foolish policy blunder that was skillfully exploited by radical leaders. Many college students came to look upon themselves as disenfranchised cannon fodder. They were old enough to fight and be killed in a war, but not old enough to have a say in their government. Before long, draft resistance and draft evasion came to be looked upon as heroic acts of integrity. Patriotism, in the old sense, was laughable, a thing of scorn.

In such an atmosphere of hostility to the government, Todd Gitlin and innumerable other people on the campuses smoked their first marijuana. It was a gesture of defiance and contempt to use an illegal drug; particularly one they believed to be harmless. Radical groups such as the Black Panthers and the Young Socialist Alliance encouraged the use of marijuana, recognizing it would further alienate the young from their own society. Later on, the filthy speech movement and the campaign for sexual liberation and the enthusiasm for slovenly clothing intentionally and effectively drove additional wedges between the young people and adults.

These are some of the primary influences that energized the radical student leadership in America's colleges. These student activists came to be called the New Left, marginalizing and displacing the older leftist radicals—socialists, Marxists and anarchists—as the principal antagonists of the social order.

"The New Left," Gitlin wrote, "became the dynamic center of the decade pushing the young forward, declaring that change was here.

50

The New Left valued informality, tolerated chaos, and scorned social order, forming the template for the revolts of hippies, women and gays." Tolerating chaos? Scorning social order? Truly, as Professor Blonsky noted, "the human psyche got altered."

Concurrent with this ferment in the attitudes of political activists in college, there were other cultural forces that reshaped the beliefs and preferences of the whole mass of American youth. Gitlin wrote, "Nothing influenced the baby-boom generation as a whole as much as movies, music and comics did. On the big screen, on posters and in popular magazines, America was mass-producing images of white youth on the move with no place to go."

Marlon Brando in "The Wild One" and James Dean in "Rebel Without A Cause" established the prototype of new anti-heroes who went looking for trouble because they had no other purpose in life. Both became idols of the youth culture. Indeed, James Dean became sort of a cult figure. A tremendous volume of fan mail was written to him for years after he died. This pattern of attractive renegades eventually included even the monstrous Bonnie and Clyde, who were presented as sympathetic characters in the film, which starred Warren Beatty and Faye Dunaway.

Far more than the movies, the popular music of the Sixties turned American young people away from the beliefs, traditions and standards of the civilized order. Rock music became the one thing that a whole generation had in common, and that bond was perversely strengthened by the distaste and disapproval of older generations. They couldn't stand the noise and were revolted by the calculated slovenliness. This is not the place to catalogue the full range of the attacks, which rock musicians directed against everything that earlier generations respected and held sacred. It is enough here to note today's immense popularity of the unspeakably coarse and blasphemous Madonna and the impassioned defenses provided for a Rap Music star who chants his advice to kill the police. As Tom Brokaw wrote in his introduction to *Life Magazine's* book on the Sixties, "A new form of popular religion flourished, the rock-and-roll church with its nocturnal, narcissistic, mischievous, anti-authoritarian creed financed by great gobs of cash offered up by faithful acolytes." Truly for many young people, Brokaw was

51

correct, music became a substitute for religion, defining and constituting what is most important in life.

A curious and unexplained aspect of the cultural upheaval is how quickly and thoroughly the guardians of the moral order surrendered their authority to the youthful rebellion. On the campuses the dormitory rules which for generations had discouraged premarital sexual activity were abandoned, as were the standards of good taste which had kept the bulletin boards and student newspapers free of gutter language, and the campus theaters free of sexually explicit films and plays. Most churches and families either were disinterested or powerless to stand against the tide of uncouth and unzippered behavior, which was tolerated and sometimes encouraged in the colleges. Probably the most crucial single default of the Sixties was the failure of government authorities to close down the giant 1969 national festival of sex, drugs and rock music in Woodstock, New York.

This was not just a mass offensive against morality and decency; it was, in fact, an insurrection, an open defiance of public law. In my judgment, the default of law enforcement on that occasion made it inevitable that drug use thereafter would be uncontrollable. In the World Series contest for dominance of the culture, Woodstock won and decency and lawfulness lost. The civil order was trampled to death at Woodstock.

Looking back now, it is clear that the schools and churches and other value-forming influences early in the 20th century had changed the basic substance of what they taught the young. Citizenship education and character education no longer were the heart of the curriculum. As a result, twentieth century Americans have turned out to be cultural orphans who were not given a full understanding of the institutions of a free society nor any idea of the importance of the principles of virtue and civility that undergird those institutions. Not understanding human nature, nor the restraints that must be imposed on human behavior in order for any common enterprise to operate, the leadership in education, religion and the government in the 1960's saw no reason to defend the established standards of civilized conduct. The problem, as Gordon Chalmers so aptly described it, was "the ethical ignorance of persons thought to be learned", who had become the leaders of the colleges and churches. When the young attacked the whole range of traditional virtues, moral authority turned out to be a hollow shell and collapsed.

The casualties of that collapse were numerous. A broad segment of vocabulary has simply become obsolete because the concepts that it embodied have been rejected. Modesty, decency, probity, rectitude, honor, politeness, virtue, magnanimity, chastity, piety, righteousness, propriety—these and many other terms of approved behavior have been consigned to limbo. They don't even enter into the calculus of public discussion and decision-making. Naturally, their opposites have suffered the same fate, terms such as vile, licentious, malign, dissolute, roué, shame, disgrace, evil, sin, stigma, ostracize, iniquity, and so on. Those designations and the concepts they represent have also been cast aside.

The American society has lost its sense of direction. Forward has been canceled. With no public consensus in support of specific ideals, virtues and principles, politics has fallen into base and tawdry squabbling. Who can out-promise whom with regard to the troubled economy? Who can curry favor with the largest number of self-serving interest groups? Who can most persuasively undermine public confidence in the opposing candidate? These are the qualifications for the most influential position in the world? America needs to find its way back to the solid ground of civilized, honorable and intelligent living. It will be a difficult journey and it will need guidance of a quality that is in scarce supply nowadays.

One sure compass for that trip back has been provided, and still is, by *The St. Croix Review.* For twenty-five years, this little magazine has presented to its readers the commentaries of people marvelously suited to lead us home. The authors include Robert Nisbet, whose books, *Quest for Community,* and *Twilight of Authority,* are prerequisites for understanding the road we must take. Alexander Solzhenitsyn, whose Commencement Address at Harvard University painfully and precisely analyzed the moral collapse of Western society, Russell Kirk, the author of *Decadence and Renewal in Higher Learning,* Duncan Williams whose *Trousered Apes* first described the brutalization of culture in the Sixties, Margaret Thatcher, the gallant head of state who forcefully commended and defended the institution of marriage, N. Scott Momaday, the eloquent American Indian novelist who understood human dignity, Leopold Tyrmand, the Polish author who, having suffered under both Hitler and Stalin, tried to help the people of the West understand the blessings and the requirements of liberty. These and dozens of other writers of principle, depth and wisdom have all been published in the *St. Croix Review.*

Angus McDonald's editorial commentary for the first issue of the publication discerned with astute accuracy the disintegration of the moral and civil order that has taken place. Here are several passages from his essay:

> From the founding of this country until some time after the war of Revolution, our thinking was dominated by religious precepts...But the clear and certain faith that religious precepts should rule society has been absent for the lifetime of every living American...The problem of society was to live in the everyday world by principles derived from a superior world. That wisdom has been lost...
>
> The abandonment of the old religious traditions has not brought mankind together into a natural and moral unity as the rationalists hoped; rather it has allowed the differences of race and nationality, class and private interest to appear in naked antagonism without any softening by religious inspiration.
>
> Under the old order, the Christian faith operated as a brake on the power of the state. Under the new order, the wisdom of religion rejected, the modern state has arisen—monolithic, intolerant, unprincipled, ignorant, and corrupt. What else could we expect when there is no recognized guiding wisdom?

Wisdom! That has been the ultimate casualty of the New Age. Wisdom, the understanding of what will be of benefit to everyone, rising above the claims of individual wants and passions, and the demands of special interest groups. The wisdom which, used to infuse the American experiment in liberty and enabled it to become the hope of the world, was drawn from the Christian heritage of the colonies as Angus noted. Morality and honesty and civility and the work ethic, all distilled from the Christian wisdom, became folkways in America and guided and benefited the lives of all Americans, regardless of their religious affiliation, if any. It is wisdom that we must resurrect in order to reconstitute decent, moral and lawful communities.

In the British Coronation ceremony, there is a point at which the Archbishop tenders a gift to the new monarch, saying, "We present you with this Book, the most valuable thing the world affords. This is wisdom." The book, of course, is the Holy Bible.

Through twenty-five years, Angus McDonald has presented an extraordinarily rich array of wisdom to his readers. An editor can do no more than that.

CHAPTER VII

WHAT EVER HAPPENED TO CIVILIZATION? THE FABRIC OF TRUST HAS BEEN SHREDDED

By John A. Howard, Counselor,
The Rockford Institute
Delivered at Carroll College, Waukesha,
Wisconsin, October 13, 1993

A story is told about a cross-country airline flight some years ago. One of the engines developed a problem and the pilot shut it off. He turned on the speaker system and informed the passengers there was no cause for concern; the plane could fly very well with three engines. Before long, another motor began to act up. Once again, the pilot turned it off, and assured the passengers that two motors could keep the plane aloft. Then a third engine stopped. Silence from the cockpit.

Soon the pilot came into the main cabin. He was wearing a parachute. "Don't anyone panic!" said he, "I'm going for help." Whereupon, he opened an emergency exit and jumped out. The moral to this little anecdote is that help isn't help unless it helps. Announcements that help is on the way are nice to hear, but if the facts of the situation contradict the reassurances, a little panic may be in order.

The time has come, I believe, for Americans to indulge in a little panic. Things are not going well. The glue that used to hold our free society together has lost its sticking power. Until about 1965, Americans could go about their daily activities in the confident expectation that the people around them would behave in a lawful and friendly fashion, or if not friendly, at least with no hostile intent. To be sure there were some individuals who were dishonest or cruel or took advantage of others, but they were so scarce there was no need to be on a round-the-clock alert, suspicious of every stranger.

That fabric of trust has been shredded. Dishonesty, corruption, vandalism, violence, crime, deceit and maliciousness have eaten into all aspects of the American reality. Distinguished universities are found to have been cheating on their government contracts. *The New York Times* printed a map of an industrial park in Boca Raton, Florida in which ten different firms in this one location were all alleged to be engaged in some from of dishonesty. Twenty-four thousand seven hundred three Americans were murdered in 1991. During that same year, there were one million, nine hundred thousand violent crimes in the United States. So many weapons are being brought to school that students in some fifty cities must pass through metal detectors as they enter the buildings.

U.S. News & World Report published an in-depth analysis of what happened in the Los Angeles riot. The interviews, court records, police radio transmissions and videotapes "show how several dozen victims were assaulted and robbed. Sometimes the perpetrators raged as they attacked passing motorists and pedestrians. Yet just as often they cheered, laughed and even danced." It isn't just a matter of harming others for one's own benefit. There is increasingly a perverse and vicious joy in causing harm. The attitudes are as alarming as the acts of aggression.

Some analysts suppose that in the economic realm it is possible to live with additional inflation every year. Perhaps that is possible. However, any thoughtful person will recognize that it is not possible for the society to survive more crime, more cruelty and more dishonesty every year. It is beginning to dawn on the citizens that the people in positions of public responsibility really don't know what to do about all this. The remedial plans and activities are not getting the job done. The help isn't helping. We are coming to a point where the citizens are taking matters into their own hands.

Consider a tragic case now being tried in the courts of Rockford, Illinois.

> Around 4 a.m. on May 10 [Peter] Chemello heard what he thought was gunfire in front of his home. Rocks had been thrown from a passing car, striking his daughter's vehicle and setting off the alarm. Chemello went outside and turned the alarm off. The car was pelted again a few minutes later. Chemello, who did not call the police, was waiting outside when the car reportedly made a third pass. He saw a brick being thrown from the car. After the car passed, Chemello went out into the street and fired at it.

This account from the *Chicago Tribune* tells of an incident that occurred this past spring. The bullet from Chemello's gun struck and paralyzed 17-year-old Jamie Hart in the fleeing car. The neighborhood where Chemello lives has suffered a great increase in crime recently. Not long before Mr. Chemello's trouble, a friend of his who lives nearby was shot when he chased some young people he believed had vandalized his car.

Many citizens of Rockford sympathize with Peter Chemello. A number of them have donated funds for his legal defense. His attorney said, "I don't want to go back to the days of the wild, wild, west, but if citizens had confidence in the police, they'd call 911. But they don't. They have no confidence and they feel that no one can protect them like they can protect themselves."

The city authorities are dismayed. Mayor Charles Box acknowledged, "There's the problem of crack, cocaine, unemployment, gangs and a general feeling of hopelessness. People feel frustrated, but we can't tolerate letting people take the law into their own hands."

Jamie Hart's lawyer expressed his dismay about the public reaction to the shooting. "It's simply appalling to me," he said, "that everybody out there is in support of this guy. People seem to think that Jamie got what he deserved. Jamie's on a respirator, his only form of communication is blinking his eyes, and he'll never have the use of his lower extremities. What a helluva price to pay... for vandalism!"

Vandalism is the intentional and callous destruction of something that belongs to someone else. It reflects the attitude of a savage who does what pleases him without regard for the rights, the feelings or the property of other people and with no sense of obligation to the community. Thievery, embezzlement, cheating, corruption in government, contrived lawsuits, indeed crime and dishonesty of every kind are forms of vandalism. All are intentional and do harm to the general well-being. The support of Rockford citizens for Peter Chemello is generated not because of anger about the damage that was done to his daughter's car, but out of a frustrated and fearful sense that the vandals are taking over and decent citizens are losing out. Prior to World War II, there were standards of acceptable behavior sustained by public expectation, by praise and gratitude and by stigma, scorn and ostracism.

For example, when I was a little child, I rode my tricycle down the front walkway of our home and out into the street. Mrs. Prindeville, driving up the block, jammed on the brakes, but the car hit me. My parents wouldn't have dreamed of suing Mrs. Prindeville. Civilized people didn't use lawsuits to get rich. Nobody else in our town would have sued Mrs. Prindeville, either. It was simply unthinkable. People in those days were raised with a conscience.

Nowadays, for many people a suit against Mrs. Prindeville is simply taken for granted. After all, she has been paying insurance to cover this kind of situation. It doesn't cost her anything extra; and the insurance company may well make some settlement to avoid the expense of a trial. With such attitudes, lawsuits multiply and so do lawyers. The rate for liability insurance goes up a notch and the cost of living does, too. And another piece of territory is lost to the vandals.

In his book, *Days of Grace,* Arthur Ashe writes of another tragic behavioral change. Concerning the brutality of the Los Angeles riots he says, "I felt sick. That's not us, I thought. That's just not us. It was as if spirits from another planet had come to earth and invaded black bodies. We were once a people of dignity and morality; we wanted the world to be fair to us, and we tried, on the whole, to be fair to the world. Now I was looking at the new order, which is based squarely on revenge, not justice, with morality discarded. Instead of settling on what is right, or just, or moral, the idea is to get even."

Conceivably, America could curtail crime, dishonesty, violence and revenge by tougher laws, harsher penalties, greatly increased police forces and more and more jails. The ruthless police state is a possibility for America, but not an attractive one, and not one that most voters would support. The only other option is to try to re-earn that status phrased so poignantly by Arthur Ashe, "a people of dignity and morality."

It is an option that will not be well received in the cultural circles of America, because so many leaders in the opinion-making activities have embraced the supremacy of individualism and the doctrine of private choice.

Morality is a system of fixed principles defining what is right conduct and what is wrong conduct. Those principles apply to everyone and are not subject to change or revocation by popular demand or by an act of Congress. In sharp contrast, values, a concept endorsed by modern culture, are like quick silver. They can squirt off in any direction, or they can simply be rejected, according to individual preference. If each person, or each group decides what is right and what is wrong, that isn't morality at all, it is ethical chaos. It is the recipe for universal vandalism. Arthur Ashe spoke of dignity as well as morality. I believe the dignity he had in mind is the solid self-respect that derives from embracing moral principles and living according to those principles.

It will be useful to consider how an attempt to reestablish morality and dignity may relate to the prevailing orthodoxies of two value-forming institutions—religion and the family—where concepts of morality are shaped and judged.

As de Tocqueville noted a century and a half ago, America's remarkably successful experiment in freedom was undergirded by the religious foundation of American life. The strong emphasis, which George Washington gave to religion in his public statements, had been continued by all his successors. The family Bible was a treasured feature of most homes, and the majority of citizens had some familiarity with it. Until World War II, the ideals of sexual morality that prevailed in America were drawn from the Bible. Both divorce and unwed motherhood were still regarded as great misfortunes and cohabitation was not socially acceptable.

Polls indicate that today a higher percentage of Americans believes in God and attends church than is true of the people in other Western nations. Even so, the authority of the Bible as the source of norms has greatly weakened. The Lord's Prayer is still a "given" in all Christian services, but if you ask a parishioner, or even a pastor, what precisely, are the temptations that the individual is asking God not to lead him into, during the Lord's Prayer, and what is the evil he is praying God to deliver him from, the likely response is one of mumbled incoherence or stunned silence.

A few passages will refresh the memory on just how specific and helpful the Bible can be in dealing with the disorders that plague the society today. The Ten Commandments prohibit murder, theft, covetousness and false witness. If that false witness ban were taken seriously, the problem of everybody suing everybody would be resolved. Three of the Ten Commandments also specify that the two-parent, male and female marriage, with intergenerational responsibility as the proper pattern for life; honor thy father and mother, do not engage in adultery, and men should not covet their neighbor's wife.

The Proverbs also bear some study. The following nine verses are taken from the First Chapter of Proverbs, King James Version.

> The proverbs of Solomon, the son of David, King of Israel...
> To receive the instruction of wisdom, justice, and judgment, and equity;
> To give subtlety to the simple, to the young man knowledge and discretion...
> The fear of the Lord is the beginning of knowledge; but fools despise wisdom and instruction.
> My son, hear the instruction of they father and forsake not the law of thy mother...
> My son, if sinners entice thee, consent thou not.
> If they say, come with us, let us lay wait for blood, let us lurk for the innocent without cause...
> We shall find all precious substance, we shall fill our houses

with spoil...
My son, walk not thou in the way with them for their feet run
to evil and make haste to shed blood.

Solomon's very name has been equated with wisdom for
centuries. Here, right in the very first Chapter, he is describing the
gangs that are devastating our cities and he says to stay away from
them. What they do is evil.

To hold aloft the Bible as the authority for what is right and what
is wrong draws the dismay and wrath of the civil libertarians and the
great chorus of other advocates of the do-your-own-thing
philosophy. "What about the Sikhs and Hindus and Muslims and
Native Americans and Zoroastrians? They have rights in America,
too! It is un-American and unconstitutional for them to have to live
in a society governed according to Jewish and Christian concepts of
virtue." So goes the attack on biblical standards.

Well, we have just witnessed a conclave of the leaders of the
many religions of the world assembled in Chicago to spread
fellowship and to proclaim a common message of reconciliation. As
it turned out, they couldn't even agree to include God in their
statement to the world. The highest common denominator that could
be achieved in that theological assembly really offers no remedy for
America's era of violence and destruction.

With biblical religion excluded, as it has been, from participation
in the efforts to deal with public questions, the decision-making is
now dominated by non-religious, or anti-religious forces. One of the
most powerful of these, *The New York Times,* has designated itself
the arbiter of what is moral and what is not. In an October 4 editorial
expressing distress about court decisions, which had taken children
from Lesbian mothers, the Times, declared, "Some children grow up
in homes where they witness or suffer physical or emotional abuse.
That's immoral. A loving relationship between two adults of the
same gender is not."

Whereas everyone can sympathize with the agony of mothers
who have been separated by judicial action from their children, that
sympathy cannot be permitted to suppress the profoundly important
question of who or what is to determine the ideals for the society and

the standards of behavior judged to best serve the large community. Is *The New York Times* a wiser and more reliable authority in these matters than Solomon, or God speaking for Himself in the Ten Commandments? The fact is that for some years, the secular forces have been redefining what is moral, eliminating most of the ancient biblical norms. Has the liberation from those standards produced a more livable society? Has that rejection of the Bible produced a nation of wise, stable, confident and friendly people?

Some forceful answers to those rhetorical questions are provided by statistics about the impact of the traditional two-parent family upon the lives of the children. The following is a quotation from a column by Mike McManus last summer. "In 1960, there were only 243,000 children [in America} living with a never-married parent. By 1990, the figure was an eye-popping 5,568,000- a 20-fold hike!...Such children are three times as likely, as those living with both parents, to flunk a grade, 3.5 times more apt to be arrested, and six times more liable to become unmarried parents themselves."

Children in households without a father are also far more likely to use illegal drugs, to have emotional problems and to have difficulty keeping a job. In her book, *The Politics of Welfare,* Blanche Bernstein, the former head of New York City's Human Resources Administration, writes, "One of the most fascinating statistics in New York is the *tiny* number of intact families receiving welfare... less than 1 percent of all intact families of 3 or more persons in the city." In New York City 99 percent of the families consisting of a father, mother and one or more children were not on welfare. The people who are self-disciplined enough and considerate of others enough to sustain a marriage turn out to be the people who can hold a job and earn a living.

Another of America's major problems resulting from the disintegrating family, was set forth by Wisconsin Circuit Court Judge, Moria Krueger. After listing the circumstances which almost always lead to delinquency, she notes, "There is just one phenomenon I know of that addresses all these needs: the need for a strong identity, for reinforcement, for structure, for nurturing, for security, for money, for status, for a moral code. All these needs and more can be and often are addressed by membership in a gang."

The gang turns out to be a substitute for a proper family. The family or the gang! Civilization or vandals! These are powerful arguments for reestablishing traditional marriage and the loving family home as ideals for American life. Of course, not all marriages are loving and lasting, nor are all parents affectionate and wise in nurturing their children, but the fact that imperfect human beings can never reach an ideal does not invalidate the importance of having a vision of what is good and striving toward it. There will always be individuals whose personal circumstances or personal preferences make it inappropriate or impossible for them to try to form their lives according to a specific ideal, but those instances should not be permitted to force the cancellation of the ideal.

In my judgment, the one change in society which would do more than any other in pushing back the tide of crime and vandalism and cruelty would be for Americans to reinstate the traditional concept of the family as the norm, the hoped-for pattern for living in the society.

It needs to be remembered that it is impossible to go two directions at once. If cohabitation, single-parenting and homosexuality become legitimized and altogether socially acceptable, then heterosexual, lasting marriage will be phased out. The principles of sexual morality required for enduring stable marriages and for honest, secure family relationships are not easily sustained under the best of circumstances. Premarital chastity and marital fidelity have been greatly undermined by the unzipped mores of the popular culture with the result that the divorce rate, like the crime rate, increases every year. Is that what people really want?

My guess is, that if America is to avoid being overwhelmed by crime and corruption and viciousness and self-indulgence, the rescue will be made by small groups and private initiatives working through neighborhoods and churches and school boards and public libraries to retrieve America's forgotten ideals and to resurrect the moral standards of a decent and dignified society.

If this occurs, you will find blacks over-represented in the leadership of the movement, for the blacks have suffered the most from the collapse of civilized behavior. Arthur Ashe is a beacon of clear-thinking about these matters. So are black scholars Thomas Sowell and Walter Williams. So is black columnist William Raspberry. So is Robert Woodson, the eloquent champion of inner-city self-help. And so is Dr. Leonard Lawrence, the President of the National Medical Association with a membership of 16,000 black physicians.

The young, also, will, I predict, be in the vanguard of that movement. The high school and college students of today have far more to lose than older generations if the vandals continue to seize more territory year after year after year. The current rates of crime and violence will look like pranks at a Sunday School picnic, compared to the carnage twenty-five years from now. You may know that this past summer a group of bright young lawyers, bankers, graduate students, writers and business people formed an organization called Third Millennium. They issued a manifesto demanding fiscal responsibility in government, improved schooling, and accountability for pollution produced by corporations. Perhaps there will arise a comparable thrust for responsible and civilized and neighborly ideals and standards. Or maybe the Third Millennium could broaden its goals to embrace those additional objectives.

The restoration of the family norm, and the revival of moral, courteous, civilized behavior may seem too difficult, may look like hopeless undertakings. That is what Bill Moyers thought in the two-hour CBS television special, "The Vanishing Family—Crisis in Black America", which he hosted seven years ago.

At the end of the show, he was interviewing a Mrs. Wallace who, with her husband, runs a community center that serves the troubled people in inner-city Newark, New Jersey. What follows is from that transcript:

Moyers: You're worried about the black family. You think it's precarious.

Mrs. Wallace: It's going to be an endangered species.

Moyers: The messages that kids are getting from the society seem to say, "Do anything you want to." The United States Government, the government of New Jersey, a white man like Moyers can't step in and say to young black kids, "It's not right to have children out of wedlock; welfare needs to be changed; you've got to take responsibility." Who's going to say these things to these kids?

Mrs. Wallace: Why can't you say it?

Moyers: They won't listen to me.

Mrs. Wallace: It doesn't make any difference; you gotta say it anyway. They may not listen to me either. But I'm saying if you say it in your corner and I say it in my corner, and everybody is saying it, it's going to be like a drumbeat. But it's not just for me to talk about, it's for us all to talk about. And it's going to surpass [people's] color. And you're not going to be safe, and I'm not going to be safe unless we send out this drumbeat.

She was right. Seven years later we are much less safe. Civilization is losing out to the vandals.

What ever happened to civilization? The teachers and the preachers, the story tellers and the playwrights, the philosophers and the statesmen, the parents and the grandparents, whose job it is to safeguard and transmit the ideals and obligations of civilized living, have failed in that duty. Perhaps the deterioration has reached the point that piety and common sense will reassert themselves. Perhaps there will be a growing chorus of people, each in his own corner, rejecting and refuting sexual liberation and the do-your-own-thing, dog-eat-dog ethic, holding aloft the things worth living for and worth dying for. I hope so.

CHAPTER VIII

WHO CARES ABOUT
THE LAWS?

by John A. Howard
President, Rockford College
at
The Law Club of Chicago
May 11, 1972

When the *Chicago Tribune*'s Walter Trohan announced his retirement and said he was going to live in Ireland, I arranged to call on him at his home in Washington, D.C. before he left. Because of his long career as a thoughtful observer of our society, I wanted to know what he considered the principal long-range concerns that a college should bear in mind as it tries to provide a worthy educational program for undergraduate students. In response to my question, he was quiet for some time and then said he thought the most important concerns all gathered under a single heading—crime. He spoke about the changed living circumstances in Washington, and his reluctance to go out into a crime-frightened city at night. He mentioned the enormous direct and indirect costs of the volume of goods and money stolen and embezzled, and the ever-more elaborate crime-prevention systems. Drugs were on his list. He concluded with an expression of doubt about the future of a society *where the youth have little respect for the law.*

Mr. Trohan's comments have come to mind repeatedly in the intervening months. Crime is not only the commission of unlawful acts. It is also a symptom of a state of mind, of a willingness to harm others for the benefit of one's self. When the rules are observed, it is possible for a group of people to take action in response to their needs and their problems, but when many people ignore the rules or make up their own rules, every problem is multiplied and the possibility of effective group action is simply a matter of chance.

What I shall do this evening is offer some comments about the consequences of a lax attitude toward laws and rules in higher education in our country.

There are many current chapters of the story, but in the weeks before the new Vietnam tensions, General Westmoreland, the Army Chief of Staff, was prevented from speaking at Yale University by the actions of angry students. At Princeton, Admiral Moorer—the chairman of the Joint Chiefs of Staff—tried for twenty minutes to give the speech he was invited to present at the Whig-Clio debating society, but it is reported that in that brief time he was subjected to 67 outbursts and hostile interruptions. What was scheduled as an informative presentation was converted into a noisy "happening." Up at Harvard, the students invaded the Center for International Affairs, breaking windows and doors and spray-painting graffiti on the walls. (I do not mean to imply that Rockford College where I serve has been without incident, but when one did occur several years ago, we took very strong action and there has been no repetition.)

Outrageous student conduct has become a commonplace, and the public seems to have become so callous about these matters that its response to campus coercion and vandalism is likely to be, "So what's new?" The society seems to take for granted conduct, in colleges, that would not be tolerated in any other organization. Try to imagine a family or a business or a bank or a law office that would put up with intimidation and wanton destruction on the part of its own members. Perhaps it is assumed that academic freedom requires the acceptance of a certain amount of barbarism in order to be genuine. Perhaps the people stand in such awe of the intellectual community that they consider it inappropriate to pass judgments on a college or a university. It really is a strange phenomenon that the citizens continue to have confidence in and send their children and their gifts and their taxes to institutions, which do not or cannot maintain even minimal standards of civilized conduct for their personnel.

In any event, I wish to suggest that the society will pay a much higher price—indeed is paying a much higher price—for unprincipled behavior in its educational community than it would in almost any other sector of civil life. Education does have consequences. We deceive ourselves if we suppose the graduates of an institution that operates without standards, except in the realm of academic performance, are not contaminated by their attendance at such an institution.

I serve as a member of the National Commission on Marijuana and Drug Abuse. The first year of our work was devoted to the study of the extent and the consequences of the use of marijuana. During that year, it became evident that with the possible exception of our armed forces, a higher percentage of college students use marijuana, than of any other group of our citizens. Furthermore, there seems to be a direct ratio between the prestige of the institution and the incidence of marijuana smoking. A professor from one of our most renowned universities testified before our Commission that about 70% of the students at his university have tried marijuana, and almost 50% are regular users— that is, they smoke pot at least once a week. (It is a paradox that education—the one agency of society devoted to the fullest use of the mind—is most heavily involved in mind-altering drugs.) Testimony from the chancellor of another university revealed that his university's published literature notifies the students they will be subject to disciplinary action if they are found to have in their possession more than one week's supply of marijuana. Apparently, some of the illegal stuff is O.K.

Wholly apart from what marijuana may do to the user, it is, I believe, a matter of far-reaching consequence that a very large proportion of the colleges and universities are conscious accessories to massive violation of public law. This circumstance has direct educational consequences. What the students are learning is that it is perfectly all right to ignore public law—if you consider it a bad law, or if you are defying the law in the name of justice, or if you are a college student.

This is, of course, a very attractive theory on which to operate. It encourages each person to believe that society must conform to *his*

71

judgments of right and wrong. The student learns to cry "foul" and demand amnesty if he is apprehended in his illegal acts. The student is encouraged to believe the laws should be made to accord with what is being done rather than with what has been officially judged to be in the best interests of society. It is this sort of thinking which sustains an argument that a law is bad because it criminalizes so many people. This line of reasoning is a non-argument. In fact, it is nonsense, for it would justify the legalization of shoplifting and auto theft. If a law is believed to be inappropriate, then the individual should work to have it changed through the properly established procedures; but just because 10% or 31% proclaim it an inappropriate law, does not make it so. There will not be *any* society if each citizen obeys or disobeys laws according to his own concept of justice. There will not be a society, just a dog-eat-dog jungle.

To some extent some campuses *have* become jungles. The takeover of a college building remains an act of uncivilized force, no matter what rationale may be advanced as a reason. To assert that it is justified because it is undertaken as a symbol of protest cannot eradicate the raw fact that it is a criminal action.

What has been the response of the academic institution when a building has been commandeered? Too often it has been to readjust the operation of the university or college to permit the invaders to retain possession of the building until they tire of their symbol and withdraw. When the smoke clears, some spokesman for the institution will then explain that the institution's laissez-faire response was the only proper course of action to avoid driving the moderates into the camp of the radicals, or to minimize the risk of injury.

Let us consider for a moment the reasoning thus presented. In the first place, it is an open invitation to the dissidents to demand more and threaten more. The child who is given his way when he throws a tantrum becomes a perennial tantrum-thrower. It is a learning process. You try something, it works, and you do it again. Of even greater consequence than the coddling and encouragement of student tantrums is the message to the other students. The message is that principle is not the basis for institutional action. Principle would recognize that the buildings have been constructed for educational purposes, and that it is the institution's stern obligation to see to it that the buildings remain available for educational purposes. Principle would say it makes no difference whether moderates, conservatives or Sunday School teachers join the invasion, the university still has the obligation to call upon such law enforcement personnel as may be necessary to remove anyone who interferes with the operation of the program. And principle would suggest the college should press full legal charges against the offenders. The failure of the university to take legal action reinforces the student's tendency not to be a stool-pigeon. This is a particularly notable characteristic of today's youth—a rigid unwillingness to take society's part in identifying one of his peers who has broken a law.

Turning to the university's desire to avoid injury, it will be recognized that this is precisely the line of reasoning that makes airplane hijacking such a difficult situation with which to deal. However, there is a vast difference between the circumstances of a hijacked plane and a hijacked building. Usually there are no innocent hostages in the case of the building. The only people who are perforce at risk are the marauders who have seized the premises, and the law enforcement officials who would be needed to remove them. The law officers are accustomed to, and trained for the risks of their profession. The students who invade a building choose not to regard themselves as criminals, but to the extent that their illegal acts are unimpeded for fear that someone will be hurt, these students are terrorists and cannot claim immunity from appropriate response to terrorism. As the spokesman for the Israeli Government noted the other day when paratroopers had repossessed the hijacked Sabena plane, if more nations would respond as they did, hijacking would become less attractive.

Interwoven with the other reasons why the academic institutions respond as they do is a widespread assumption that it is somehow improper for a college or university to concern itself with laws, or to ally itself with law enforcement officers. For many academic minds, laws are tainted because they involve judgments and are rigid in nature, both qualities being deemed antithetical to "true" intellectual processes. This, I know, sounds strange to the outside world, but the theory seems to be that whatever a scholar does is worth doing

73

because it is a scholar who does it. Nonconformity must not only be tolerated, it is to be championed.

What has happened is that many academic institutions have become one-dimensional operations. Their single basis for action is the protection of the unrestricted play of the mind. This characteristic was documented by a study conducted by two University of Minnesota professors, Drs. Gross and Grambsch. They sent questionnaires to 10,000 administrators and faculty members at 68 universities, both public and private. They asked the professors and administrators to put in order of priority what they believe *are* the purposes of the university, and on a second list, what they believe those purposes *ought to be.* More than 7,000 usable answers were received. When tabulated, they revealed that the number-one objective on both lists was "To protect the academic freedom of the faculty". Ponder that! The means have become the ends! What happens to the student is a secondary concern, if indeed it is regarded as having any importance at all.

This same one-dimensional phenomenon is, of course, observable in the withdrawal from the campus of any regulations or norms that could possibly be construed as operating *in loco parentis.* At many institutions, it is a point of pride that no judgments are made or even offered about student conduct. This attitude of the modern college not only invites students to play games with witchcraft and revolution and cohabitation and drugs and shoplifting-as-a-sport, but it also encourages the student not to set limits on his own conduct, not to pass judgments on anyone else's conduct, and to regard his own mind as the supreme guide for his actions. This is the training ground for the do-your-own-thing devotee. This is the apprenticeship for the person who looks the other way when his neighbor commits a crime, and protects the identity of the criminal when someone tries to investigate. This is the learning situation, which produces the arrogant youngster who accuses adults of not listening to him if they fail to agree with him, or if they do not make changes to accord with his perception and desires. And the saddest part of this youthful attitude is that the student usually *believes* it is simply a matter of a failure of adults to listen. If the world does not respond to his drum, then the world is deaf or callous or stupid.

The generation gap created by such an education of the youth is very real at this period when the *older* generations were trained to believe that personal limitations and personal obligations are natural and necessary parts of living in a society. It is more than a generation gap. It is a generation chasm and it may be of such proportions as to be unbridgeable. The lyrics of one of the popular songs of today identify the dimensions of that chasm. The song entitled "Chicago" says in part, "We can change the world, rearrange the world", and then there are some words about freedom, followed by "rules and regulations, who needs 'em?" Freedom is perceived as the absence of rules.

Let me take this point a step further. Recently our Drug Commission visited Spain and Greece. The incidence of drug abuse by the citizens of those two nations seems to be very low, with the exception of certain young people who have frequent contact with tourist youth. I asked the Spanish and Greek clinicians, psychiatrists, doctors, law enforcement and government personnel and others with whom we visited, why they thought their citizens did not use illegal drugs in contrast to neighboring countries. The answers were almost all the same—a strong family structure with strict rules and a deep sense of familial obligation, a strong church, which requires much of its parishioners, and a respect for law. These people are disciplined by an education from family, church and state, which builds both character and citizenship.

It is interesting to discover how when one makes any favorable comments about Greece or Spain in our country, he often stirs up some angry or condescending comments about repressive governments and freedom. There are many dimensions of freedom. When we were in Madrid, we had a meal with three Rockford College girls who are taking their junior year studies in Spain. They told us they could go to any part of Madrid, day or night, without the slightest fear of being robbed or molested.

A survey taken in the United States more than a year ago noted that half of the women and one-fifth of the men in our country are afraid to walk outdoors at night. Our people are prisoners in their own homes after dark.

Which nation has freedom?

The latest official estimates of the number or heroin addicts in this country run between half a million and a million, with the probability that the million figure is closer to the actuality. What more cruel prison is there than heroin addiction? Compared to a population with only incidental heroin addiction, are we the free ones?

Please don't mistake my intent. I am not suggesting we exchange our government for theirs, but I am suggesting that our nation seems to go along with giant blinders, deluding ourselves with the supposition that *we* have it made, and the problems we face are temporary aberrations or maladjustments which will soon be dealt with by the automatic genius of a so-called free nation. We are concerned about crime and drugs, but many people seem to think these problems will soon be on the mend. Somehow.

It simply is not so. If the educational system has taken a wrong turn, then the whole society will soon be trailing along down the same path, for today's undergraduates are tomorrow's movers and shakers. If the young have little regard for the law, it will be a confused world when they are running it.

Education in *most* societies is, and always has been, a process of acculturation, of helping the young to learn how to live *acceptably* and successfully in the society. Much of American higher education has completely and intentionally discarded any such effort. The result of abandoning citizenship education is a decline in citizenship. The result of abandoning character education is a decline in character. The result of placing the individual intellect on the highest pedestal of academe is to leave the young adrift on a sea of confusion without the compass and the rudder of the wisdom distilled from man's experience. Man has learned the hard way what is required for people to get along together, and that learning has been codified in public laws and morals and mores. These are rules of conduct that have to be instilled in the young. If we fail to impart these codes to our children, it is they who are the primary victims. We are seeing the consequences of this failure to teach the rules reflected in a massive epidemic of illegal drug abuse among the young people.

There are, of course, many factors, which influence the young people to try drugs, but I am convinced that by far the greatest impetus for the young to use drugs is their desire to ease the pain of the purposelessness and cynicism and the loss of confidence in the institutions of society, resulting in a cosmic forlornness. These attitudes have, I believe, been generated by an educational system too heavily dominated by relativism and the new morality, and by a corollary absence of specific limits and obligations derived from principle and conveyed to the young with deep conviction.

The one-dimensional college, committed primarily to a one-dimensional service will appoint a revolutionary or a nihilist to the faculty if the academic freedom *of the faculty* is the supreme guide, and the individual under consideration is qualified in his scholarly field. Indeed, the institution is obliged by its own priorities to hire him.

On the other hand, if a college should concern itself with educating for responsible citizenship, as Rockford College tries to do, then the person committed to destroying our form of government and the person espousing law-breaking to achieve his ends, is simply not qualified to teach at that institution. He couldn't possibly teach the students to be responsible citizens of a democracy. The difference in these two views of education is a difference of extreme consequence. In the one case, the revolutionary is hired and is then free as a teacher to spread his poison among the students and to use his talents to subvert and thwart any efforts to help the students understand and support our form of government. He is free to encourage and coach the students in shouting down a responsible military commander invited to explain our military policies. The appointment of the revolutionary to the faculty implies that his views and his statements are just as valid as any other professor in providing wisdom and counsel and understanding to the students. By its own policies, the institution teaches the importance of non-judgment.

Winston Churchill once said he had no difficulty in choosing between the fire and the fire engine. The dominant orthodoxy in higher education not only will not choose between the two, but makes a virtue out of the absence of the choice.

We should not, I believe, be surprised if crime increases rapidly

77

in an era when the youth are educated to place their own judgments above the dictates of the law, and when the faculty includes individuals whose professed aim is to destroy the rule of law.

In conclusion, let me repeat. Education does have consequences. It seems to me your profession needs to give some careful thought to what sort of citizens our colleges and universities are training.

CHAPTER IX

THE MARIJUANA PROBLEM

Persuasion At Work
Vol. I, No. 2
April 1978[13]

Among the simmering public issues, one, which has attracted minimal public partisanship within the business community, is the question of marijuana and other illegal mind-altering drugs. The new laws decriminalizing marijuana use in several states cannot fail to generate additional problems for the businessman and everyone else with a stake in a lawful and productive society.

"This One's Clean—He's On Grass"

A recent cartoon in the *Richmond News Leader* depicted the apprehension of two smokers by two burly officials in HEW uniforms. One officer, holding a man in hippie garb, reported to his partner, "This one's clean—he's on grass." This satire of Secretary Califano's anti-smoking campaign highlights the corrosive civic confusion resulting from the nation's unwillingness, or inability, to take a stand on marijuana. The prevailing assumption seems to be that if we can dispense with harsh punishments for using the drug that will solve our marijuana problems. Wrong.

In the first place, a 1977 Gallup Poll reported that 53% of the population favored decriminalizing marijuana use, but 63% of the

---

[13] Monthly publication of Rockford College (March 1978-February 1987).

people were opposed to legalizing the drug. The result of trying to accommodate both preferences is bizarre. California has revised its statute so that while it remains a misdemeanor to smoke marijuana, punishment is restricted to a fine. All other misdemeanors in the state carry a possible jail sentence. It is not in the nature of law to contradict itself.

Furthermore, decriminalization of marijuana will have the direct result of proliferating crimes of a far more serious nature. As the penalties against use are minimized, the demand for the drug multiplies, leading to an increase in cultivating, importing, transporting and selling marijuana in commercial quantities. These activities remain felonious crimes. The number of smugglers will increase, new channels for bootlegging will be opened and the containment of contraband, which is already a difficult task, will become still more troublesome.

Already the pressure is building to move on from the decriminalization of use to the legalization of the production and sale of the drug. For this step, the obstacles cannot be overcome by a mere manipulation of public opinion. The United States is joined in an international pact, which pledges the member nations not to legalize marijuana. The International Control Board, supported by our government and more than seventy others, has taken the flat position that marijuana is harmful to both the individual and the society. It is noteworthy that many of the signatory nations have had centuries of experience with this drug, whereas in the United States, use was limited to a tiny segment of the population until just fourteen years ago.

The Champions of Decriminalization

The direction in which we are heading on this matter is clarified by the nature of the forces leading the decriminalization campaign. The effort is spearheaded by the National Organization for the Reform of Marijuana Laws. It chooses to call itself NORML, a clever gambit of ideological warfare. Founded in 1970 by Keith Stroup, a Washington D.C. attorney who still serves as its director, NORML has a full-time staff and has established chapters in various states to sway public opinion and enlist legislators in behalf of diminished penalties for marijuana use.

The sixth annual meeting of NORML took place in the nation's capital last December. The conference sessions dealt with the standard fare of such gatherings— the alleged relative harmlessness of the drug, the civil rights of drug users, "horror" stories of mistreatment by police and the courts, therapeutic benefits that have been identified for glaucoma and pain relief among certain cancer patients— but the overriding theme of the membership was, " We like to smoke pot and we don't want to be arrested for it." (Many did smoke pot during the meetings, even in the presence of speakers and panelists who were federal officials, and were not arrested for it.)

Emotionalism, shallow reasoning and a flat assumption that marijuana laws are to be ignored characterized much of the commentary from the floor as well as some of the platform presentations. Insults and obscenities greeted any speaker who dared to disagree with the pro-marijuana thrust, and one such speaker was assaulted with a pie. In that particular session, an officer of the government spoke of the international barriers to legalization. The point was greeted with vocal displeasure from the audience, the gist of which was, "Who cares about international treaties? We want to have the right to smoke pot."

In a statement to the conference, Director Stroup left no doubt that decriminalization is but a way station to larger objectives. "It does cause me some pause when the President of the United States now has the same official position towards marijuana that we do. It kind of says something to me. Number one, I'm glad to have his support, but number two, I think it is about time we began to get out a little further ahead, and begin to point the direction for where we should be headed." This comment was greeted with shouts of approval.

The "Pot" Culture in Print

The activist efforts of NORML are reinforced in print by a number of publications, the most impressive of which is a slick monthly magazine called *High Times.* The March issue contains 116 pages including thirteen full-page color ads for drug paraphernalia, with other full-page promotions of grow-your-own psychedelic mushrooms and pot, a deodorant spray for neutralizing marijuana odors, *Playgirl* magazine, NORML of course, and equipment to be used against wiretapping and bugging. Among the celebrities openly cited as users of various illegal drugs are author Susan Sontag, tennis star Vitas Gerulaitis, and Jean Paul Sartre. The feature story, signaled by Fidel Castro on the cover, is a detailed account of the tourist attractions in the cities and provinces of Cuba. One article deals explicitly with the extensive use of drug themes in rock music. *High Times* touts the books it has published, the latest of which is entitled *The Pleasures of Cocaine.* The centerfold presents a young lady on a mountain of marijuana. For advanced decadents, there is a write-up of Chris Burden, the so-called conceptual artist who has had himself crucified on a Volkswagen and shot in the biceps, complete with a color photo of the blood dripping down his arm. The guest editorial, railing against informers as the enemies of justice and liberty, is provided by Richard Ashley who is credited with writing frequently for the *New York Times* as well as *High Times.*

It is hard to appreciate the utter contempt for the norms and standards of society, which characterize the publication and the activist organization at the forefront of the pro-marijuana movement without reading the one and observing the other in conclave. If the nation follows such leadership, it is hazardous to predict our destination, but it is not likely to resemble civilized or productive living.

The Foes of Decriminalization
There are, of course, vast numbers of more moderate citizens who favor marijuana decriminalization, as well as their counterparts who oppose such action, but there is a telling contrast between the NORML-*High Times* axis and the most vigorous anti-decriminalization forces. The hard-line opponents unwittingly identified in the NORML conference turned out to be the responsible leaders of inner-city and ethnic groups. A black California legislator, although jovially alluding to his own hedonism, told the NORML audience that he could not have introduced a Sacramento bill to decriminalize marijuana cultivation for private use if his district had had a larger black population. He emphasized the point by citing the

mayor's veto of a decriminalization bill in Washington, D.C. in response to heavy pressure from some of the city's black leadership. A New Mexico state senator admitted that despite his own inclinations, Mexican-Americans do not generally favor decriminalization.

These comments call to mind the current efforts of The Reverend Jesse Jackson to persuade the students of inner-city high schools to stay off illegal drugs so that they can make something of themselves; and they echo testimony presented to the National Commission on Marijuana and Drug Abuse that every black and Puerto Rican legislator had voted against a bill to liberalize the marijuana laws in New York State. Experienced observers of the inner-city identify specific hazards that marijuana poses to the young people, e.g.:

1. Although it seems to be proven that there is nothing inherent in marijuana which impels an individual to move up to "hard" drugs, nevertheless if the person's motive for smoking marijuana is a mechanism to escape from difficult and depressing circumstances, marijuana is not very effective for that purpose so that the escape motive, coupled with access through marijuana channels to other illegal drugs, may well lead to the use of heroin or other more powerful "highs";

2. The flashy affluence of the dealers in marijuana is a powerful lure to inner-city youngsters to turn to illicit careers in contrast to the seemingly more difficult paths to a better life.

The Big Question: Decadence and Self-Indulgence vs. Discipline

The almost uniform anti-marijuana stand of the respected spokesmen of groups struggling for a livelihood, juxtaposed with the pro-marijuana thrust of more affluent people who simply enjoy getting high, poses in microcosm the cultural challenge to our society. Shall the enthusiasm for unrestricted self-indulgence led by the liberal and radical chic communities prevail? Or will there arise some leadership with the vision and the courage to face up to the requirements of a rational, lawful and responsible society? Must the inner-city population, which faces many disadvantages, be subjected to this additional jeopardy solely to please the whims of the more privileged groups in society?

A realistic appraisal of the reigning attitudes in the press, the academy, the church and the legislative halls provides little encouragement to hope that responsible leadership from these quarters will develop an effective response to the festering marijuana problem. The business community may be the only influential force left in the nation that still operates on the basis of assessing dispassionately the relative merits of conflicting claims about an important problem in order to pursue a course of remedial action. In this instance, corporate America has much at stake. Increasing crime and dishonesty are the predictable consequences of the growing marijuana decriminalization movement. [Not only has President Carter endorsed national decriminalization but also so have Dr. Robert Dupont, director of the National Institute on Drug Abuse, and Dr. Peter Bourne, Special Assistant to the President, on Drug Abuse. (*Parade,* December 11, 1977, p. 16.)] Puerto Rican, Mexican-American and black leaders have registered their unequivocal judgment that "pot" is the enemy of those who would rescue themselves from poverty. Here is an opportunity for corporate leaders to register dramatically the good faith of their desire to assist their less fortunate neighbors. And, finally, the marijuana issue is a logical point to take a resolute stand against the powerful cultural forces spreading the do-your-own-thing poison that is vitiating the discipline, the lawfulness and the industriousness requisite for a sound and productive society.

CHAPTER X

ADDRESSING THE DRUG PROBLEM INTELLIGENTLY

An address to the Rotary Club
of Madison, Wisconsin, February 13, 1985

Those of you sufficiently ripe in years to have studied Greek mythology in school may recall the fate of Sisyphus, the King of Corinth, who was condemned to push a great boulder up a hill, only to have it roll back down, whereupon he must try again eternally. For years, it has looked as if our society was doomed to the same kind of endless and futile labor as we have tried to contain the problems of drugs, crime, ineffective schooling, inner-city hopelessness, and other manifestations of profound social disintegration.

Over the past eight and a half years, our studies at The Rockford Institute have led us to believe that many of the tribulations we suffer and much of our incapacity to deal with them stem from a lack of understanding about human nature. We have ignored how human beings usually interact with one another. We have not considered the obligations that each person must accept in order for any group to live together amicably and productively.

Recently there have been encouraging signs that a more accurate view of human reality is surfacing at critical points in the idea industries. If that understanding takes hold, we could be on our way to higher ground. I want to share with you a glimpse of some of those favorable omens, but first I think it is important to try to examine in some detail one example of the tragic shortsightedness, which has governed our well-intentioned efforts to deal with large problems.

John A. Howard

Doped-Out America?

Today's lesson is in the realm of drugs—illegal, mind-altering drugs. Everyone is aware of the movie stars, sports heroes, and pop musicians whose careers have been shattered or whose lives have been lost in the drug culture. Almost daily we read of the arrest of traffickers or the seizure of vast quantities of one illegal drug or another. We all have at least some impression that we face real trouble with drugs.

Let us try to bring the matter into a sharper focus. In 1978, the U.S. marijuana crop was estimated at a billion dollars. The harvest last year is believed to have been worth more than 16 billion dollars, second only to corn among American crops. Seventeen months ago, *Newsweek* summarized a national study sponsored by our government, which calculated the annual cost to the society of illegal drugs to be at least 25 billion dollars. Of that total, five billion was the cost of the police, the courts, and jails in dealing with drug cases. The employers present will be particularly interested that another five billion was lost to absenteeism, blunders, slowdowns, and sick leave in the work force. Please remember that that figure does not include problems with alcoholic beverages.

In the *Wall Street Journal's* feature series on drugs last November, it was reported that despite the extensive campaign mounted by the government, it appears that cocaine imports have increased by 50 percent in the last two years. You may have seen Governor White of Texas on a recent MacNeil-Lehrer report somberly calling for much greater Federal efforts to block the drug traffic into the southern tier of states.

A few days earlier, Jacques Cousteau and his son provided a heartbreaking report of how the demand for cocaine, largely from the United States, has resulted in crime and corruption in the countries that grow the coca plant and has led to rapidly increasing cocaine addiction among the natives, who for centuries have only used the drug in a mild and relatively harmless form.

Last August, the governments of Bolivia, Colombia, Ecuador, Venezuela, Peru, Panama, and Nicaragua issued a joint declaration condemning drug-trafficking as a crime against humanity. A recent article in the Knight-Ridder newspapers stated: "The drug problem

86

has reached such proportions in Latin America, officials say, that it is threatening not only the economies, the social well-being, and public health, but national stability as well." The Organization of American States has scheduled a special meeting about illegal drugs seeking some effective joint action.

There is, in short, disquieting evidence that the incapacity of the United States to contain its drug problem has caused vast and devastating new problems in Latin America which, alas, already has more than its share of economic, social, and political difficulties to address. To wrap up this overview, I ask you to ponder a statistic cited by Cousteau: each day 5,000 people try cocaine for the first time.

Futile Efforts to Stem the Flow

It isn't that the United States hasn't been trying to stop the flow. On the contrary, we have mobilized the Coast Guard, deployed hundreds of sniffing dogs, trained the customs inspectors to recognize the signs of nervous traffickers, set up a special task force headed by the Vice President, and initiated countless other enforcement activities and educational programs. Yet cocaine imports have increased by 50 percent and marijuana is on its way to becoming our largest crop. Things aren't going well for us on the drug battlefield.

Actually, that failure is not surprising in view of the nature of our anti-drug campaign. The major effort is to try to intercept the drugs on their way to the user. That is not an intelligent way to go about it. The trouble is that the market works. Since there is no effective reduction in the demand for drugs, the amount of money available from those who want to use the drugs is so great that no matter how many Coast Guard cutters, border patrols, and sniffing dogs we mobilize, human ingenuity is going to find ways to deliver the drugs over, under, around, and through these barriers, even at the risk of incarceration or loss of life. Some people are always willing to jeopardize their careers or lives for vast fortunes. The market works. Interdiction of drug traffic does not, and cannot.

If the people of the United States truly wish to have the government involved in diminishing the use of mind-altering drugs, there is a technique that does work. That involves the imposition of major penalties for the possession of any amount of the illegal drugs. When Spanish law set the penalty at six years in jail for possession of one marijuana cigarette, Spaniards simply didn't use marijuana. Other nations have used this method with remarkable success. So has the U.S. Navy, which, under the leadership of Admiral Thomas Hayward, instituted a policy of no tolerance. That program hasn't had much play in the media, but it has been dramatically effective. And aren't we glad that it has! The thought of a bunch of potheads manning our weapons is unnerving. You will recognize that if the demand for drugs is substantially curtailed, we won't have to spend enormous sums in a futile effort to apprehend the traffickers.

I am not a lawyer but I believe it isn't necessary to wait for the Federal government to apply this remedy. I believe any state or municipality could enact its own statutes against drug possession. Such action will provoke an outcry from the drug users and civil liberties purists. We should remember, though, that every law that is passed imposes a restriction on individual liberty. Moreover, the drug problem has reached such a magnitude that some very hard decisions must be made about what we are prepared to sacrifice in order to try to bring it under control.

Moral Relativity's Triumph

Now we have come to the difficult and sensitive part of this analysis. When I served on the National Commission of Marijuana and Drug Abuse more than a decade ago, we were twice scheduled to visit Turkey to try to persuade that government to do more to diminish the Turkish cultivation of poppies, which are the source of heroin and also the major crop of many Turkish farmers. Those visits were canceled because our State Department was engaged in some sensitive negotiations with Turkey and didn't want to compromise them with our discussions about poppies. At the time, it struck me as strange that the United States government should try to pressure other governments to penalize their citizens for producing drugs when we are not willing to legislate user penalties sufficiently stringent to minimize drug usage. That doesn't make sense. It is arrogant and unjust.

In the realm of individual behavior, the American society has lost the capacity to judge certain behavior to be right and the opposite behavior wrong. Our drug laws provide a glaring example of this moral paralysis. We have recognized the devastation caused by drugs but we can't bring ourselves to say, "You mustn't use them." We avoid that moral judgment by going after the traffickers, usually justifying such action by the feeble argument that they are luring children into drug use.

What we are looking at is a cultural failure of staggering dimensions. The principal idea industries—and they are literature, the movies, the press, commercial entertainment, the academic community, and religion—for the most part reject normative standards for individual behavior so long as individual conduct does not harm someone else. Moral relativity has triumphed.

Both history and reason tell us that no group of people can live together or accomplish anything if each person does whatever he pleases. The result is chaos. There must be standards of conduct, which are determined by the group, insisted on by the group, transmitted by the group to each new generation, and reinforced by penalties imposed for failure of observance. This requirement of a society has somehow faded from the knowledge and understanding among the cultural forces that control American thinking and American policies about education, the laws, the family, and the whole range of our social institutions. The harvest of that shortsightedness is our inability to cope with crime and drugs, neglected children, and so many other social tragedies.

A New Dawn of Understanding

At last, we have come to the upbeat part of my remarks. There is a new dawning of understanding in the idea industries that gives promise of a saner and more humane future. There is a growing recognition that we must reconstitute a public philosophy embracing not only the minimal requirements of truthfulness, lawfulness, and integrity, but reaching out to include the acceptance by each individual of his share of responsibility for the common well-being. I will touch on just two examples.

Not long ago the National Endowment for the Humanities issued a powerful statement urging the reestablishment of the transmission of our cultural heritage as the central part of the curriculum for our schools and colleges. Let me quote from that text. "The humanities tell us how men and women of our own and other civilizations have grappled with life's enduring fundamental questions: What is justice? What should be loved? What deserves to be defended? What is noble? What is base? Why do civilizations flourish? Why do they decline?" Without widespread knowledge of how the brightest minds of the past have responded to such vital questions, we will continue to flounder around, governed by policies based on what is popular rather than what is wise. It is encouraging that Dr. William Bennett, who was chairman of the governmental body, which published that report, is our new Secretary of Education.

Another promising development. Last Thanksgiving Day, 27 scholars issued a statement documenting the need for all of our schools to engage in formal programs of character education, teaching the young their obligations as civilized individuals and responsible citizens. This document and the one from the National Endowment for the Humanities are worthy of study by all school boards, college trustees, and everyone else concerned about what is taught to our children.

To conclude, we have paid a large price for the shortsightedness of those opinion leaders who have given us an era in which standards of behavior and civic virtues are no longer even considered in the thinking about our laws, our courts, our schools, our literature, our families, and the other influential elements of our common life. The mass catastrophe of a drug culture out of control is but one of the sad consequences of that lack of vision. We can rejoice that there is a growing body of thought leaders who clearly recognize that standards of behavior are essential to any organized group, be it family, an athletic team, a business enterprise, a community, or a nation. The challenge is to encourage those thought leaders when they surface, make them known and appreciated, and support their efforts so that their message will eventually be woven back into the policies governing the institutions through which our common life is conducted.

CHAPTER XI

THE TRADITIONAL FAMILY UNDER ATTACK AND SOME SUGGESTIONS FOR REVERSING THE TREND

by
Dr. John A. Howard, President - The Rockford Institute
for Williams Bay (Wisconsin) Women's Club
April 16,1981

At the baptismal ceremony for our son, the minister, having taken the baby from my wife, said very quietly to the people in attendance, "What I hold in my arms, good friends, is God's greatest gift, a new life. This child, at this time, is a wonder of potential. How that potential may develop, for better or for worse, will mainly be determined by the people gathered at this altar, the family. I charge you to remember that the shaping of this life is in your hands, and I pray that with God's help, you may encourage and cultivate that which is good and kind and wholesome, and discover and set aside that which is self-centered and corrupt and destructive in the environment you provide for this child who has been entrusted to your care and nurture."

How that child's potential will develop. "For better or for worse," he said. A seemingly simple choice, but, oh, what an important one! Important for the child, and for all those people whose lives will be touched by his. That shaping of the young life identifies the joys and the great rewards of parenthood, and also the obligations incumbent upon the father and mother— the awesome and permanent and holy obligations which those parents bear. That "for better or for worse" also identifies the crucial importance of the family to the survival of a free society. Let us think for a minute how the rearing of the child affects two different kinds of society. In a totalitarian country, it makes little difference how the child is treated in the home. He is molded and programmed by state indoctrination, propaganda and terrorism. The totalitarian government rules that life by dictate and coercion. In a free society, however, where each person travels where he will, fulfilling his life according to his own priorities, moods, and skills, it is critically important for the society that the individual citizens achieve emotional maturity and sound and affirmative goals for their lives.

It is obvious that every human being has inclinations and passions, which, if allowed free rein, can lead to self-destruction and social havoc. The difference between the barbarian and the civilized man is that the barbarian is governed by his passions, doing whatever comes into his mind, whereas the civilized person subordinates his passions so that he may achieve his goals in a manner that permits him to live in reasonable harmony with other people.

A person has to be taught to be civilized. This is not a process that automatically happens. If an individual reaches adulthood without self-discipline, it is very difficult for him to learn at an advanced age how to get along as a cooperative and contributing member of a group. Teaching values and civilized conduct to a grown-up is not easy. On the other hand, it is altogether natural for the very young child to learn, from the beginning and as he grows, the wholesome necessity of accommodating and postponing some of his desires to fit in with the pattern of family requirements and priorities. Through this process, the child can come to understand and accept duty, humility, sacrifice, generosity, integrity, kindness and all the other components of social maturity. The recurring conflicts of interest among the family members introduce the child to the tensions of the larger society, but it is an introduction in which the child may achieve *in a wholesome and loving environment* the crucially essential balance between self-respect and cooperation, that eternal push-pull between what I want and what the group needs.

We have been considering the family as a training ground for the concepts and patterns of behavior that the individual must accept if he is going to be able to live comfortably with himself and with other people in a free society, things that are best transmitted within a loving family environment. It is with such thoughts in mind that some of the wisest commentators of our time keep pointing out that the free society cannot survive the disintegration of the traditional family.

The degree to which the American family is coming unglued is well known, but let us consider just one statistic. For several years, more than half the children born in Washington, D.C. have been the offspring of unwed mothers. This is the highest percentage among the big cities, but others are not far behind. Common sense tells us that some of those mothers will manage to raise their children in a manner that will give the kids a chance to be responsible and productive members of society, but a great many of those mothers, perhaps a large majority, will not. If we think we have trouble today, try to imagine the frequency of vandalism, shoplifting, rape, robbery, arson and so on when those millions of unfortunate youngsters are out on the street. When that time comes, we may well look upon today as a peaceful paradise compared to the social chaos we will then face.

So we have a problem. What can be done to repair and revitalize the family? What can you and I do? Isn't this such a massive thing that it can only be attended to by powerful people in far off places? No, I don't think so. I think thoughtful people need to speak out publicly for the principles we consider important.

I would like to identify several principles that I believe are basic to every solid and lasting family, but which have somehow been upstaged by the noise and glamour of the new psychology and the new morality. Let us begin with the principle of commitment. The tentative marriage is virtually doomed from the outset. The storybook romance wherein the starry-eyed couple lives happily ever after is an attractive figment of the imagination. It simply doesn't happen in the real world. The enduring happy marriage is available only to those who work at it and continually make sacrifices to sustain it. The strains and stresses on the relationship between any two people living in close quarters will be numerous and occasionally intense. The partial commitment— one that is made with some reservations, with a planned escape route if it doesn't work out—that partial commitment tends to be eroded by the inevitable conflicts between two people, conflicts which multiply after the children are born. The comprehensive commitment, "for richer, for poorer, in sickness and in health 'til death do us part," made and *earnestly intended* in the presence of God and the assembled company, is the keystone of the family structure. Anything less than that harpoons the marriage before it ever begins.

The liberalization of divorce laws has been one of many public policies that undermine the family as an institution. Formerly, the laws reinforced the concept that marriage is a crucially important commitment, which could be dissolved only under certain circumstances and with the concurrence of the court after a careful review of the situation. Now, in a number of states, the importance which officialdom places on the wedding bond has been reduced to the level of a clause in an automobile insurance policy. Marriage is just another contract. In case of accident, there is a no-fault easy out. However casual the driver or the spouse may have been about his or her responsibilities, there is no reason to be concerned, for the legislature has removed all obligations and all guilt. Nobody is held accountable. It is, I suggest, only as we resurrect the principle of commitment and restore it to a position of highest prominence that we will begin to repair the damage that has been done to marriage. My daughter attends a church in another city, where the minister insists that an engaged couple complete a three-months' marriage preparation course with him if they are to be married in that church, and he counsels with them regularly for a year thereafter. Over a period of eleven years, there have been only two or three divorces among the one hundred and fifty couples who have said their vows at that altar. That clergyman and his very fortunate parishioners have a clear understanding of the importance of the marital commitment.

Let us turn to a second principle, the principle of authority. Pure democracy, like living happily ever after, is a romantic dream. It might work in the camp of the saints, but it is simply inoperable among mere mortals. The effectiveness of any group depends upon the allocation of responsibility to those most capable of fulfilling it. We need to remind ourselves that there is nothing wrong or shameful when mature judgment prevails over unseasoned judgment. Every parent will scramble to keep his little child from running out into a busy street. Nobody would insist that the parent and child should have equal votes about whether the kid should be a traffic hazard. Nevertheless, with increasing frequency parental judgment concerning the activities of teenage children has been withdrawn at the very period in life when the sap rising in the loins tends to befuddle whatever judgment the youngster may have developed. There is a natural hierarchy in the sequence of generations. The family is founded upon the judicious exercise of authority by the older generations and the willing acceptance of that authority by their children. This, after all, is the substance of God's Commandment: Honor thy father and thy mother. The good Lord did not waffle on this. He did not say only until the age of fourteen, or only when you agree with your parents. This is a principle. And if the father and mother have, themselves, genuinely accepted the authority principle as set forth in the First Commandment, trying to observe the rules for living which God has make known, then their advice will be wise and useful for their children. The Ten Commandments, after all, form a package. You can't extract three or four that serve your purposes and ignore the rest, and have a life or a society that amounts to much.

Let me offer one other observation about this subject. As one who has worked professionally with young people for more than thirty years, I can tell you that the teenager whose parents have backed away from holding him to ideals and standards of conduct, that youngster is tragically deprived, and in many cases the child senses this deficiency and recognizes it as a failure of love as well as a failure of judgment on the part of the parents.

Closely allied to the principle of authority and essential to its proper fulfillment is another concept, the moral principle. It is nothing but a decisive recognition that there is an unbridgeable gap between right and wrong. The blurring of moral distinctions brought about by the seductiveness of the so-called "New Morality" has poisoned every aspect of human interaction. The government, the economic system the educational institutions, the medical and legal professions, social services, the church, and above all, the family have been crippled because of a moral climate in which each person has been encouraged to decide for himself what is OK and to behave accordingly. This rejection of fixed and eternal rules of conduct has not only rendered our social institutions ineffective and unreliable, it has also taken a terrible toll on the human psyche. The psychiatrists' couches, the alcohol and drug rehabilitation centers, the mental hospitals and all the chic groups for trying to pump up one's ego are populated with individuals who cannot stand the oppressive burden of a nothing-is-good-and-nothing-is-bad existence.

It is only in the context of moral distinctions that marital fidelity, loving and effective disciplining of the children, gentle and patient care for elderly relatives and all the other obligations that are elements of the family at its wholesome best can be sustained. When there is no over-arching sense of moral duty, *gladly fulfilled*, when each person indulges his whims of the moment, then it isn't really a family at all, but a job lot of individuals who happen to be related.

The manner in which a person goes about doing his part to reassert these principles in his own home and in the larger society must vary according to individual capacities, but there are courses of action available. Some time back it was reported that a small chain of stores in another part of the country decided to remove the grossly immoral magazines from its news racks. When word got around, these stores had a significant increase in customers, people driving extra miles to patronize a business that was willing to stand up and be counted in the arena of what is right and what is wrong. Do you suppose there are stores in your neighborhood that could be persuaded to cleanse their news racks?

In any effort to limit the availability of periodicals, there will be shrill voices that condemn the action as a violation of the First Amendment. Freedom of speech and freedom of the press will be used as bludgeons to smash the effort and bring public scorn upon the participants. However, it must be remembered that whereas the

Constitution guarantees the right to speak freely and to publish materials, it does not guarantee the right to force people to listen to or read or take seriously the pronouncements of anyone else. Such coercion is the hallmark of tyranny, not liberty. School officers or publishers or proprietors of bookstores have an absolute right, if not an obligation, to judge what will be excluded in the written materials involved in their professional activities. Benjamin Franklin understood this critically important distinction. When he was urged to print in his newspaper allegations about individuals that he judged unproven or slanderous, he refused to publish them in his paper, but offered to print them at the expense of and under the name of the person who wished to publicize the allegation.

It is, I suspect, largely because the general public has been ferociously and falsely badgered whenever it resisted objectionable material that good people have remained silent and inactive as the outpouring of amoral and even blatantly degenerate subject matter has increasingly taken over the movie and television screens, the stage, the magazines and the literature of our society. What we read and see and hear does affect our values and our behavior. Irving Kristol once wrote:

> After all, if you believe that no one was ever corrupted by a book, you have also to believe that no one was ever improved by a book (or a play or a movie). You have to believe, in other words, that all art is morally trivial and that, consequently, all education is morally irrelevant. No one, not even a university professor, really believes that.

The codes of conduct required to sustain the family are all under relentless pressure from cultural forces that scorn those codes and persuasively advocate conduct of a very different nature. What needs to be done is not only to try to diminish the advocacy of moral anarchy, but—and this is even more important— to multiply in the cultural fare the stories and instances of people who do live by principle and sacrifice for principle and are admirable models of civilized behavior and worthy family participation.

In our country, most of the people who know better have stood on the sidelines, as one after another, the principles of our social institutions have been challenged in the public forums, then berated and belittled and finally cast aside in favor of exactly the opposite concepts. And now we stand confused and frightened amid the consequences. The pastor said it all at the baptism: "I pray that with God's help, you may encourage and cultivate that which is good and kind and wholesome, and discourage and cast aside that which is self-centered and corrupt and destructive in the environment you provide for this child who has been entrusted to your care and nurture." As a nation we have not delivered very well on that invocation. And the family is only one of the victims of that national failure.

CHAPTER XII

UNDERSTANDING WHAT'S GOING ON

by
Dr. John A. Howard, Director
Rockford College Institute
At a private luncheon for business executives in
Hartford, Connecticut
February 6, 1980

Jacques Cousteau has introduced his television audiences to a world which everyone knew existed, but which few people could picture except in the unreliable realm of imagination. I wish to present to you a glimpse of another sector of reality that is about as little known as the undersea depths, but is of critical and immediate importance to the business community.

My subject is the vast interlocking network of organizations and publications that seek to replace private enterprise with some form of socialism, or are devoted to more narrowly focused goals but ones which, in their accomplishment, will profoundly cripple business operations.

For openers, let me call your attentions to the August 27, 1975 issue of *Take-Over*, a periodical published in Madison, Wisconsin. This particular issue focuses upon kidnapping as the means to finance radical activities. It presents a list of 40 corporate executives proposed as prime targets for large ransoms. In addition to the names, the article provides addresses, and the amount each corporation can pay in ransom, calculated according to the formula, which had been used in arriving at the sixty-million dollar figure, which revolutionary kidnappers in Argentina received for the ransom of the Borne Brothers. The Eastern targets include Reginald Jones of General Electric, Maurice Granville of Texaco, John DeButts of AT&T, Frank T. Cary of IBM, and Charles Peter McColough of Xerox. Another article offers a scenario for kidnapping Ray Kroc of McDonald's. The seizure of Mr. Kroc is projected on a one-way street, which he travels daily at an early morning hour. The paper also quotes Abbie Hoffman to the effect that political kidnapping is the wave of the future, and cites Chairman Mao's warning that you shouldn't kill the hostage since it only makes him a martyr and you don't get the ransom. A box headline asserts, "It is the people's money and it is up to you... to return it to the people and to yourselves."

It sounds crazy, doesn't it, like a sick joke. This can't really happen in the United States. Well, friends, this publication is real. It is one of the more extreme among about a thousand papers and magazines published in the United States, all of which are devoted to goals that in one way or another will damage the private enterprise system. Who are the people who produce these publications, and how did they get that way? You will, I presume, recall the reports of young people, mostly college students, traveling to Cuba in their summer vacations, ostensibly to help harvest the crops. Well, Cuba, like Libya and Russia, has long engaged in indoctrination programs to train foreign cadres and commandoes in the justification, the rhetoric and the tactics of what they call liberation movements. The effectiveness of such indoctrination can now, perhaps, be believed by the American public after seeing in action the product of such training, the so-called "student militants" who seized our embassy in Iran. It must be evident to the most uninformed mind that what happened in Teheran was not a spontaneous outbreak led and sustained by amateurs. These are people highly skilled in Marxist tactics and international psychological warfare. Psychological warfare is something entirely different from mere advocacy promotion or rebuttal.

Let us look back a little further into the radical surge in the

United States. Most of us recall that the Students for a Democratic Society, or SDS as it was popularly known, was an organization of impassioned student militants who wrought havoc on campuses across the country. The damage which they caused to buildings, equipment, library card catalogues and to the very fabric of civilized living was just as unreal and unbelievable then as *Take-Over*'s advocacy of kidnapping is some years later. What happened on the campuses was wanton destruction on a massive scale. The American ethos is such that the citizens simply could not comprehend the magnitude of that devastation, nor the twisted fervor of the minds which engaged in it, so although this nation-wide phenomenon was observed, it was never really understood in terms of the passionate alienation which it demonstrated and the vast number of young people infected with this plague. Thus, when SDS went out of business in 1969, there was a general assumption that that horrible chapter was finished and we could, thank goodness, get on with business as usual.

Unfortunately that wasn't the case. The broken pieces of SDS didn't just get absorbed into the flow of things but, as in some science fiction thriller, they remained active agents, progressively contaminating the institutions, the traditions and the norms of virtually every aspect of our society. At its peak, the SDS had about 100,000 members fervently committed to rendering America a Marxist state. The issue which split asunder the 1969 SDS convention was whether to escalate the use of violence, or whether to work to bring about the revolution through the existing institutions and channels of change. Most of the hard-line partisans of violence, who were numerically insignificant, went underground to form the Weathermen's organization, which engaged in sporadic bombing, arson and some kidnap plots. The Symbianese Liberation Army of Patty Hearst fame was another fragment of the violence faction.

A large portion of the rest of the SDS members, tens of thousands of them, have pursued their ideological goal with varying degrees of intensity in hundreds of organizations promoting social, political, religious and economic change. There is scarcely a militant movement of today that does not derive much of its intellectual justification, its tactics and its momentum from SDS alumni who serve as leaders and/or theorists. The targets for their highly sophisticated attacks include the nuclear energy industry, all corporations which do business with South Africa, the CIA and FBI, the J.P. Stevens and the Nestle corporations, the oil industry and multi-national corporations. The intensity of this assault should be of concern to the whole business community.

Let us put a little flesh on the bones of that assertion. Take the anti-nuclear thrust. The War Resister's League, an old-line leftist organization that had concentrated its efforts on unilateral disarmament by the United States, used its extensive communications network to assemble delegates for an anti-nuclear conference in Philadelphia in April of 1977. Out of that meeting came a new organization called Mobilization For Survival. In December of 1977, eight months later, the fledgling Mobilization For Survival sponsored a conference at the University of Chicago attended by representatives of 144 organizations from 34 states. They laid plans for the sit-ins and protests on specified dates at designated nuclear plants in different sections of the country. Each conference participant was given a protester's portfolio. Notice how thoroughly these people were prepared for this campaign. The materials each one received included the categories of anti-nuclear arguments that would appeal variously to church groups, parents and other segments of society. Other leaflets provided an antinuclear rationale based on human rights, an outline of the evils of capitalism and the blessings of socialism, and there was a manual on how to organize a church or a community in behalf of the cause. There was also a guide on "How to Fascinate the Press." Please register on that term "fascinate." It is not facts and logic that were stressed, but how to command public attention—this is, as we noted, psychological warfare, not winning a rational argument. Just as in the case of the seizure of the Iranian embassy, the anti-nuclear protests in America have not been spontaneous reactions, but media events orchestrated by highly sophisticated, impassioned and formidable opponents.

A new wave of organized and very sophisticated protest is swiftly developing in reaction against the proposal of registration for the draft. This week's issue of *The Militant*, which is the weekly tabloid of the Young Socialists' alliance, carries the headline:

"THOUSANDS PROTEST CARTER'S DRAFT—We Won't Die For Exxon." This is not a naive organization. It clearly understands the difference between draft and registration: the confusion of the two is intentional. And notice that the whipping boy is American business—"We won't die for Exxon."

I said that the young revolutionaries of the sixties have fanned out into organizations fighting *against* one target or another. They are at least as numerous and influential in the militant movements, *advocating* this, that and the other fundamental change which they believe will weaken the structures of capitalistic America: the legalization of marijuana, gay rights, consumerism, environmentalism, nationalized health care, the abolition of tests in school and college, abortion, and the Equal Rights Amendment, among many others. In these matters, too, the track record is one of impressive, precisely calculated long-range planning and exceedingly skillful manipulation of the media, and above all, the enlistment of innocent and well-meaning individuals and groups in behalf of the cause.

Let us turn to an example of how effective these radical efforts are in obtaining support from people and groups that do not understand what they are helping. The National Organization of Women, or NOW as it is called, held a national conference on the future of the family, in New York City last November. The program was a part of a much larger campaign to mobilize support for the Equal Rights Amendment, which involved the cooperation of thirty-three women's magazines all of which used their November issue to push hard for ERA. The printed program for the NOW conference begins by defining a family as "two or more people who share resources, share responsibilities for decisions, share values and goals, and have commitment to one another over time.... regardless of blood, legal ties, adoption or marriage." Let me underscore that last phrase, "regardless of blood, legal ties, adoption or marriage." The ERA is seen as the vehicle for restructuring the family and the place of work in conformity with this definition of a family. The intent is to provide women with a legal right to all the privileges and perquisites of a career while engaging in whatever sexual arrangements they choose for any period of time, *with full family*

103

benefits for the live-in partner. The campaign also calls for federal funding of child care.

Among the speakers and panelists at the New York conference were the perennial radical, Dr. Benjamin Spock, the grand duchess of sex education and sexual liberation, Mary Calderone, and radical philanthropist, Stewart Mott. Ninety-five organizations were listed as co-sponsors of the conference, ranging from the Association of Junior Leagues and the General Federation of Women's Clubs to the most powerful radical organization in the country, which is the Institute for Policy Studies. In addition to the co-sponsors, there were 35 sponsors who seem to have paid for the conference. They include Quaker Oats, McDonald's, Kraft, General Motors, General Mills, Celanese, Cargill, Avon, and Connecticut General Life Insurance. Given the consistent radical stance of the NOW organization and the ideological slant of most of the speakers, it is amazing how many people, organizations and companies were persuaded to support this conference. From the point of view of those who wish to destroy American capitalism, consider the probable level of personal stability and productivity of a future work force which, from childhood, has been reared and acculturated in a "home" environment where the family has no legal or moral responsibilities and no permanence—an eternal sequence of temporary sexual liaisons.

I trust you are all aware of the anti-big business campaign that Ralph Nader has recently launched, sponsored by his new consumer-labor coalition. It involves the advocacy of the Corporate Democracy Act of 1980, which proposes to regulate industry in ways that will radically affect the conduct of your business. However, that push for new laws is only the tip of the iceberg in his campaign to circumscribe and discredit big business.

The coalition of organizations that I mentioned earlier mobilized against nuclear energy is trivial compared to what will be the massive array that can be expected to support Mr. Nader's anti-capitalist drive, which is scheduled to culminate in programs and demonstrations throughout the country on April 17. In the first place, Ralph Nader can probably count on the full participation of Tom Hayden and Jane Fonda and the organization they head, called the

Campaign for Economic Democracy. Tom Hayden, you will recall, wrote the manifesto to launch the SDS, and served as the SDS president. In the recent Hayden-Fonda tour of fifty cities to promote their organization, they received at every stop publicity beyond anything that has happened since Charles Lindberg returned from Paris.

The union leaders Nader has already enlisted are formidable in the clout they carry. One of the initial labor sponsors is Douglas Fraser of the UAW. According to *The Dispatcher* (Sept. 8, 1978), Mr. Fraser gave a speech on July 19, 1978 in which he said, "I believe leaders of the business community, with few exceptions, have chosen to wage a one-sided class war today in this country— a war against working people, the unemployed, the poor, the minorities, the very young and the very old, and even many in the middle class of our society." The head of another union backing the Big Business Day is William Wynn, head of the United Food and Commercial Workers. Mr. Wynn stated, "Just as the 1950's scrutinized the labor movement, and the 1970's, big government, this day will mark the 1980's as the decade to correct the abuses of big business."

The Advisory Board listed on the Big Business Day stationery lists all the usual leftist cause trumpeters: Julian Bond, Cesar Chavez, Barry Commoner, John Conyers, Ronald Dellums, Michael Harrington, Fred Harris, Robert Heilbronner, Arthur Schlesinger, Jr., and many others. The list also includes some championship flight troublemakers: Jeremy Rifkin, whose People's Business Commission offered $25,000 in reward to the secretaries of major corporate executives if they provided proof of wrongdoing which led to the conviction of their bosses; Timothy Smith, the brains behind the anti-corporate activities of the National Council of Churches; and Richard Barnet, a co-founder of the Institute for Policy Studies. I mentioned that organization earlier as the most powerful and dangerous in the country. Time does not permit me to try to explain its power and reach, and all the radical organizations and publications in which it is involved, but there is a description of its operations on pages 50 to 57 of *The Alternative Media*, the book which we have published.

The *Rolling Stone* magazine, which is the *Wall Street Journal* of the teenagers, is such an enthusiast for Nader that it chose to celebrate its 100th issue by featuring a very long interview with Mr. Nader in which he explained how he would dismantle private enterprise. Most people haven't any inkling how the phenomenon of rock music/pop music has operated as a vehicle for radicalizing the nation's young people, for encouraging them to reject the values and the norms and the institutions of the free society, including private enterprise.

The initial suggestions for a business response to Ralph Nader's anti-capitalist blitz provide sobering evidence of how profoundly the business community misunderstands the nature and the power of its antagonists. Herbert Stein suggested in a *Wall Street Journal* editorial that big business shut down on April 17 to show the country how vital big business is to everyone. Another suggestion has been to retaliate with an anti-big labor campaign. Either of these projects would, I assure you, be turned enormously to the advantage of your opponents, as they trumpet the liberal theme that the businessmen who care nothing for the working people and the poor, wield their immense power only for their own self-interest.

What is needed, I believe, is a carefully devised, massive and sustained national campaign to make known to the country what are the proclaimed objectives of the leaders and the organizations, which are mounting the attack. If the citizens truly understood the specific long-range goals of your most potent critics, I think the people would react strongly against them, and for you. The trouble is that, as happened with the NOW conference in New York, citizens in every field of endeavor, including the businessmen, don't understand what is going on, nor who is manipulating public opinion, and how, and why, and so they respond unwisely to the challenges skillfully devised and brilliantly orchestrated by highly sophisticated agents of radical change.

In these few minutes, I have only scratched the surface of the array of organizations and publications that are now at work in the United States attacking and undermining not only private enterprise, but also the church, the family, the military, the laws, the educational system and all the other institutions which make it possible for a free society to exist and to be productive, and to be just plain livable. The SDS, when it was in business, mounted intemperate attacks on the systems of the free nation with no clear idea of how the society could operate in the absence of those systems. They simply were out to destroy what they didn't like. The poison of this adolescent reaction to vital social mechanisms has now spread to literally thousands of groups that are eager to rally to each other's causes. Come April 17, the business community will have all too clear an idea of just how far this process has gone.

May I suggest to you that in the cultural arena—that is, the battleground where attitudes and opinions are formed and changed, and passions are crystallized—in the cultural arena, the businessmen are firing marshmallows from slingshots, whereas the opposition is using live bullets in their machine guns and they have a vast arsenal of ammunition in reserve. The most astonishing aspect of this unequal contest is that one side really doesn't have much of any idea what is going on.

This is not, I suggest, a situation in which the answer is to assemble the public relations officers and instruct them to attend to this problem. By and large, public relations personnel both by training and by inclination are ill-equipped for this task. Their primary responsibility is to please people, to make new friends and to minimize frictions. First, the problem must be thoroughly understood and then strategies must be devised by *specialists* who are steeped in the knowledge of the activist movements and who know how to take advantage of the substantial vulnerabilities of these movements which they have so far very effectively kept hidden.

I am grateful for the opportunity to present to you some vital information and our interpretation of it.

CHAPTER XIII

FEDERAL AID: STAMPEDE TO DISASTER

Rockford College *Widening Horizons* Newsletter
April 1963

A story is told of a motorcycle driver who, on a wintry night, reversed his jacket so that the bitter winds would not come through the gaps between the buttons. The jacket was somewhat uncomfortable back-to-front, but it served the purpose. As he sped along the road, he skidded on an icy spot and the poor fellow crashed into a tree.

When the ambulance arrived the first-aid men pushed through the crowd and asked a man who was standing over the victim what happened. He replied that the motorcycle rider seemed to be in pretty good shape after the crash, but by the time they got his head straightened out he was dead.

So it goes when people get excited and take quick action to provide a remedy for a problem without clearly understanding what the problem is. Now we are being rushed into ill-advised remedies for education which violate the nature and neutralize the vitality of the educational system that has ably served this country's needs under circumstances the most various. The qualities of the educational system, strength or weakness, wisdom or folly, diversity or uniformity will inevitably be reflected in the society some years later. As we may undermine the effectiveness of our schools and colleges, we circumscribe the potential of our society.

The title of these remarks, Federal Aid to Education: Stampede to Disaster, makes use of strong terms. They are intentionally arresting. It is my belief that we as a nation are unwittingly placing in jeopardy our entire system of education and that the tocsins of alarm must be sounded so loudly and so frequently that the people and their representatives in Congress and even the educators, themselves, will think through the consequences of the course we now pursue and change its direction.

What is a stampede? It is a rapid mass movement. It is engaged in thoughtlessly. It is caused by fright. It is dangerous, and it is exceedingly difficult to stop. The press toward Federal subsidy of education, in my judgment, meets precisely each of these qualifications.

Except for a few lonely voices, the men and women in our Federal government when they turn their attention to education are discussing not *whether* the United States Treasury shall pay more of the costs of education but rather which costs and in what manner. On January 29th of this year President Kennedy issued a White House Message on Education. "Our concern as a nation for the future of our children," said the President, "and the growing demands of modern education which Federal financing is better able to assist make it necessary to expand Federal aid to education beyond the existing limited number of special programs."

The requested expansion is set forth in a single comprehensive bill entitled the National Education Improvement Act of 1963. It is "aimed at meeting our most urgent education problems and objectives, including quality improvement; teacher training; special problems of slum, depressed and rural areas; needy students; manpower shortage areas such as science and engineering; and shortages of educational facilities." The program proposed seeks Federal funds to meet all of these problems and more.

Shortly after the President's message, Republican members of the House Committee on Education and Labor reported in a news conference that they would propose legislation of their own to provide Federal funds to meet the problems of education. Even before the President's message, more than one hundred and twenty bills affecting education had been introduced in this Congress. The most influential educational associations of America are all on record repeatedly urging the Federal Government to provide money for buildings, scholarships, research and many other items including, in some cases, faculty salaries. The mass movement aspect of the Federal aid stampede is an assertion that will be readily granted.

The charge that it is a thoughtless movement will require more elaboration. Let us take an example of what passes for thinking among the advocates of Federal subsidy of education. Recently there appeared in the *Princeton Alumni Weekly* an article entitled "The Blessing That Is Federal Aid." It was written by McGeorge Bundy at the behest of Princeton's President Goheen.

Mr. Bundy, you will recall, had served for some years as a Dean at Harvard before joining the White House staff of advisors. If anyone is in a position to phrase convincingly the argument for Federal subsidy of education, it is this man who is one of the key formulators of national policy and who has the perspective of substantial academic and administrative service at our most renowned university.

His proof of the blessing rests on four points. The first is that Federal funds allocated to higher education have been productive. None would be foolish enough to contradict his statement that Federal funds have been productive. They have indeed been productive. Who could spend a billion and a half dollars a year on anything without producing quite a lot of something? The question is not "Have Federal funds been productive?" It is instead, "How productive in contrast to the same amount of money from other sources and what have been the by-products?" A claim that much has been accomplished begs the issue.

Dean Bundy's second point is no more relevant than his first. He states that Federal funds produce freedom in education because if the scientist and the scholar do not have the funds to carry on their work their poverty limits their freedom. The Federal monies certainly do liberate scholars to practice their profession.

Again the logic is incontrovertible, but the argument completely misses the mark. The Federalness of the money, which is presumably the bone of contention, is totally unrelated to the fact that the funds received by the scholar free him to do his work. Any money, regardless of source, does as much.

Mr. Bundy's final two efforts to prove the benefits of Federal educational subsidy are: a claim that the restrictions governing the use of Federal funds are fewer than those that govern the use of money from other sources, which is arrant nonsense, and a claim that the method of determining the operational details of Federal educational programs is more in keeping with the great academic tradition than is the method of determining the nature of programs paid for by funds from other places. Here he refers to the practice of asking representatives from a number of educational institutions to assist in planning programs subsidized by the Federal government. This process assures that the standardized programs subsidized by government represent the best thinking, or at least the best compromises, that can be obtained from the most highly regarded scholars in a given field.

An admirable practice it is if you must have standardized programs, but it is certainly not in the American academic tradition wherein each college or university plans its own programs according to its own specific opportunities and limitations.

These four points constitute the proof offered by Presidential Advisor Bundy that Federal aid is a blessing. If this were an isolated example of justification for Federal aid by something less than thought, it would be necessary to support further my contention that the Federal aid movement is an unthinking stampede. However, this is about as effective a case as has been made and Princeton's president must have so judged it for he presented it to his alumni apparently in an effort to qualm their fears about Federal funds.

Except in the case of those people who candidly seek to centralize all functions of society, there is not any sound argument for using Federal funds in preference to other funds.

The third characteristic of a stampede is that its cause is fright. A whole new Federal invasion of education was launched in response to the great fear that struck on October 4, 1957. Sputnik the First sent a chill into the hearts of all of us. The startling realization that Russia had outdistanced us in space technology rocked us as a nation. We were suddenly willing to grant new powers to government and suppress historic and well-reasoned objections to certain Federal activities, out of plain, old-fashioned fear.

The National Defense Education Act of 1958 put into being vast new programs some of which can be labeled "defense" only by an interpretation of the word so broad as to render it meaningless. Furthermore, it seems as if the fright is being perpetuated by many who are committed to Federal support of education. The President's message, already referred to, closes with the recitation of Soviet superiority in the number of scientists produced each year. The implication is clearly that we cannot hold our own in the Cold War if the legislation is not enacted. The Federal aid movement is urged on by scare techniques and the stampede gains momentum.

Before we consider the consequences of this movement, let us turn back the clock fifteen years when President Truman proposed a similarly sweeping program of Federal legislation to pay educational costs. The storm of protest he aroused, although now largely forgotten, demonstrated a degree of unanimity on the part of educators at all levels seldom witnessed before or since. Typical of the comments of that era was a statement by President Gould of Carleton College.

"I miss no opportunity to reiterate my opposition to Federal aid for education. As a matter of fact, the more I talk about it and the more I think about it, the more serious does that threat become. It is almost stupefying that intelligent people cannot see what may happen if we continue to promote movements in that direction."

Joining Dr. Gould in the opposition were the presidents of Columbia, Northwestern, Stanford, Brown, Beloit, Grinnell and a host of others. These were not the narrow-minded reactionaries of the period but the most highly respected statesmen of their profession. Theirs was not a newly conceived attitude. Listen to another statement issued in March 1945.

> The first purpose of this document is to warn the American people of an insidious and ominous trend in the control and management of education in the United States.
>
> For more than a quarter of a century and especially during the last decade, education in the United States, like a ship caught in a powerful tide, has drifted ever farther into the dangerous waters of Federal control and domination.
>
> This drift has continued at an accelerated rate during the war.

Present signs indicate that unless it is sharply checked by an alert citizenry, it will continue even more rapidly after the war.

It is the deliberate and reasoned judgment of the two educational commissions who join in the appeal which this document makes to the people of the United States that the trend toward the Federalizing of education is one of the most dangerous on the current scene.

The quotation comes from a joint report issued by the problems and policies committee of the American Council on Education and the educational policies committee of the National Education Association. These two committees were speaking, in effect, for the whole power structure of American education.

It is to be wondered what has taken place in recent years to bring about a complete reversal of the firm position of the educational leadership of our country. The principles which underlay earlier objections remain intact. No new discoveries have outmoded the principles. I am suggesting here that the principles have been disregarded in the stampede, and that we will be unutterably foolish if we do not return to principles as the basis for action in meeting educational problems.

The new thinking which buttresses the clamor for Federal subsidy cheerfully rejects principle as a primary consideration. In a book published last spring, *The Federal Interest In Higher Education,* the authors candidly recite a list of fictions that were introduced by the Congress in order to obtain the passage of educational legislation. Several brief quotations from that volume illustrate this astonishing point.

"In general, the potentially divisive character of the issue has been avoided by the creation of a number of polite fictions which allow the substance of the legislation to be considered without too much argument over its implications for the separation of Church and State. Such adjustments are not made without a price being exacted somewhere. Sometimes the price has been the excision of program elements that could not be covered by the agreed-on fictions, and at other times the price has been the setting of precedents that encumber future action..."

"As we have said, there is nothing inherently wrong with such fictions. Indeed, in cases like the one just cited, they allow implementation of what a majority feels to be desirable social policy by providing an honorable way to avoid a contentious issue. The difficulty is that ruses good for one set of circumstances may not be good for—indeed, may be positively obstructive to—another set..."

"In a broader sense, it is surely true that no society—in the world, at least—has ever been able to afford the luxury of facing squarely all the issues that divide its people. The use of fiction as an instrument of cohesion is an indispensable social tool."

The authors of these incredible statements are Dr. Homer Babbidge, who was until recently, the Assistant United States Commissioner of Education and Dr. Robert Rosenzweig, an Assistant to the Commissioner of Education. Their book is considered by many the most authoritative and convincing presentation of the case for Federal aid to education.

What, ladies and gentlemen, have we come to when dishonesty, or fiction, which is a politer but nevertheless synonymous term, is engaged in by the congress to hoodwink the people into the acceptance of programs, which would be rejected on principle?

Now let us examine some of the reasons that underlie the traditional rejection of the Federal Government as the means of support for education. In the first place as the Federal Government becomes the largest single source of funds for college after college, and there are a number already in this category, the institution becomes beholden to the government.

This is not a chimera born of a doctrinaire distrust of government. Recently I wrote to the president of a large well-known university inviting him to join a group of college presidents in making known the arguments against the ever-growing Federal subsidies of education. He replied that although he was in full agreement with our position that the subsidies are not in the long-range best interests of the colleges or the country, his own university was now so dependent upon funds from Washington that he could not exercise his rights as a citizen on this issue without jeopardizing the university he served.

Think about that answer, if you will. The mere flow of Federal money has silenced the opposition. This loss of freedom on the part of those who depend on government for their income was the reason for refusing suffrage to the residents of the District of Columbia.

Let us project the Federal aid programs ahead, not too many years the way things are going, to the time when *all* colleges and universities will receive the largest part of their budget from the United States Treasury. Is it possible that all faculty members in that day will feel some obligation to vote for whichever party promises the largest amount of additional educational subsidies regardless of other partisan differences? This is not an unlikely result. Political freedom is sacrificed by those who depend upon government resources. Can we afford to sacrifice the political freedom of the whole academic community?

Earlier we referred to the by-products of Federal programs of education. First let us be quite clear that there is no need to depend upon conjecture for ascertaining the effects of Federal funds in education. I recently received a manual of almost eight hundred pages devoted to a brief description of each of the educational programs in which the United States Government now engages.

As a matter of fact, college executives may now subscribe to a periodical solely devoted to the presentation of new Federal programs, and new interpretations or changes in old programs. Indeed the scope of current Federal programs offers plenty of opportunity for observation.

The current issue of *Nation's Business* contains an article describing the overlapping, the inconsistencies, the distortions and the general confusion, which characterize the aggregate of government educational programs. The source of information for that article is John F. Morse who has just completed a nine-month study for the Higher Education Subcommittee of the House of Representatives. I commend to you Mr. Morse's statements. The inescapable conclusion seems to be that we must have a Washington superauthority to make plans for the academic segment of our society and to coordinate as well as pay for education through a central bureaucracy. This will be the disaster referred to in the title.

The predominant characteristic of American higher education has been its diversity. Each collegiate institution has its own particular nature, totally distinguishable from every other. The degree to which spiritual concerns affect the student during his undergraduate years ranges on different campuses from predominance to insignificance. Similarly the political impact upon the student varies from pure conservatism at one college to extreme liberalism at other institutions. The curricula are varied to a much greater extent than is generally recognized. Scripps College in California and St. John's in Baltimore place primary emphasis upon the humanities. Antioch in Ohio and Northeastern University in Massachusetts plan studies to support directly intermittent vocational experience.

Programming of class schedules, the division of the academic year into time units, the presence or absence of fraternities, the size of the town, the percentage of students who carry jobs, the mores prevalent on the campus, and the strength of the student government are just a few of the many variables which color and mould student attitudes and vary the scope of student knowledge, totally apart from the nature and persuasiveness of the particular teachers in whose classes the student enrolls.

As graduates of these various institutions come together in any enterprise bringing with them their own views, their own bands of knowledge, their prejudices and their experiences, that enterprise is the livelier and the more creative for the variety in its constituent personnel. I subscribe to the hypothesis that it is this convergence of diversely educated people in a free interchange of thought that has been the one condition which more than any other has enabled our nation to make the achievements it has in commerce, in culture, in comfort, and in all the other aspects of our society.

What fosters this diversity? Principally it is the autonomy of the various institutions. As a college executive conceives or receives a new idea that seems promising, he has to sell it to only his own faculty and board of control. If he can convince them that it is a sound project and can find the financial resources to implement the plan, it is tried. The innovations of each college will arise out of its own peculiar circumstances, the particular strengths of the faculty, the philosophical objectives, the limitations or the advantages of the facilities, and, yes, the personal biases as well as the imagination and courage of the President and his governing board. It is the independence of each collegiate body that fosters diversity.

Each new educational undertaking of the Federal government reduces the diversity of American education. Indeed, I believe most college executives would agree that those programs now supported on our campuses by Federal funds could be carried on at least as effectively by a comparable amount of funds from other sources, and in many, many cases could be conducted with more creativity, more imagination, more flexibility, less bother and at a much lower cost if the funds came from the traditional sources. Given such an agreement, why then do not the same executives oppose Federal aid? The answer is money.

Money is a good servant but a dangerous master. Money becomes the master when it takes precedence over other considerations. The reason that it is so difficult to justify Federal aid to education is that apart from an outright philosophical commitment to the centralization of the services of society, the only justification for Federal aid is a lack of money, and the awkward, fact that the Federal Government is far more prodigal with its funds than are other sources. If only the proponents of Federal aid would come right out and state this fact, we could face the issue head on and measure what the easy money buys against what we must sacrifice in order to obtain it.

It is undeniable that our increasingly technical society requires an increasingly skilled and knowledgeable population and, to accomplish this end, a larger part of the gross national product must be invested in education.

The issue is whether this urgent objective is to be achieved through congressional action-which forces the people to pay more for education and at the same time diminishes the diversity and circumscribes the creativity of the separate colleges-or whether the nation can be persuaded to provide the necessary funds through the traditional sources and thus preserve the freedom and the strength of American education.

The latter course takes hard work. Fund-raising is often a frustrating and thankless task, but no priceless asset is earned or retained without labor and sacrifice.

I cannot believe that my colleagues in college administration would so readily forfeit the full potential of their respective institutions, nor would shirk the task of local financing if they fully realized what was at stake. As bleak as their financial future may appear to them, it cannot be the reason for abandoning integrity. The course of educational statesmanship is to protect the greatest creative potential and the greatest institutional individuality. I don't believe that course lies via the Federal Treasury.

The college executives and the officers of government who may have a part through their silent or vocal support of Federal subsidy will have to answer to history for the consequences of their position.

May this nation recognize in time the stake it has in keeping education decentralized and unfederalized. If these views make sense to you, I urge you to do everything in your power to defeat any forthcoming educational subsidy bills and also to increase the flow of funds to higher education through other channels. The accomplishment of both objectives is essential to the strength and vitality of the nation.

CHAPTER XIV

ENNOBLING OBLIGATIONS
YOU MAKE A LIFE
BY WHAT YOU GIVE

By
John A. Howard, Counselor, The Rockford Institute
Delivered at the Mount Holyoke College
Sesquicentennial Program, Chicago, Illinois,
October 23, 1987

In 1933, *Within This Present,* a novel by Margaret Ayer Barnes, received the Pulitzer Prize. The story begins in 1914 in a spacious and elegant Lake Forest home where the family has gathered in honor of the grandmother's seventieth birthday. After the dessert was served, the birthday celebrant, Mrs. Sewall, startled everyone by standing up and announcing she was going to give a speech. "I thank God," she said, "that I can still feel young and uncertain and perplexed, yet undaunted, just as I did at sixteen. Of course I see a great many things in life that perplex me. And what perplexes me most is that I can't understand how they came to be there—in my life—in our lives, I mean. You see, we've changed. The family... We're not at all like what we started from. I've seen it happening for fifty years and still I don't understand it. We've gained some things, but we've lost others. On the whole, I think we've lost more than we've gained... We've lost the things I should have thought most likely to endure."

What had somehow been lost during the Sewall family's journey to wealth and high estate was the moral fiber, the indomitability, the spirit, which had brought an earlier generation as pioneers to Chicago and which had carried the senior Mrs. Sewall and her late husband through the loss of their home and their business in the Chicago fire. Those of us sufficiently seasoned to remember the good-humored spunk that was called forth among millions of American families during the Great Depression, are, like Mrs. Sewall, bewildered that the changes we have seen during our lifetime have included an apparent reduction in the dauntless determination to make things turn out OK, in the number of people who, in Mary Lyon's terms "will go where no one else will go and do what no one else will do." Puzzled by that lapse, we are grateful to Mount Holyoke for designing this sesquicentennial celebration to shed light on this shadowed corner of the American psyche.

Brian Griffin speaks of "the ineluctable incandescence of the human spirit." He calls it "the mystery...the desire to be good. It is," he says, "the secret knowledge that only by being good can we become joyful." For many Americans of recent generations, the knowledge of that prerequisite of joy has remained all too secret. That isn't altogether surprising because there are so few efforts nowadays to kindle the moral spark among the young or even to let them know that such a thing exists.

In *The Closing of the American Mind,* Allan Bloom writes of the impact of what he sees as the contemporary university's moral agnosticism.

> The souls of young people are...spiritually unclad, unconnected, isolated, with no inherited or unconditional connection with anything or anyone. They can be anything they want to be, but they have no particular reason to want to be anything in particular. Not only are they free to decide their place, but they are also free to decide whether they will believe in God or be atheists... whether they will be straight or gay... and so on, endlessly. There is no necessity, no morality, no social pressure, no sacrifice to be made that militates going on, or turning away from any of these directions.

One hundred fifty years ago that was not the case, as the early documents of Mount Holyoke certify. An unpublished statement Mary Lyon wrote in 1835 to make known the nature of the proposed seminary concludes with the sentence, "We hope to redeem from waste a great amount of precious time, of noble intellect and moral power." The mobilization and transmission of moral power is clearly at the core of the educational design enunciated for the Mount Holyoke Seminary in the published bulletin of 1837. The text begins:

This institution is established at South Hadley, Mass. It is to be principally devoted to the preparing of female teachers. At the same time, it will qualify ladies for other spheres of usefulness. The design is to give a solid, extensive, and well-balanced English education connected with that general improvement, that moral culture, and those enlarged views of duty, which will prepare young ladies to be *educators* of children and youth, rather than to fit them to be mere teachers, as the term has been technically applied.

Later in the booklet, there is an explanation that gifts raised by the institution will enable the students to attend at a relatively modest fee. That subsidy, "comes to them as a high and valuable testimonial of the estimate in which are held the services of female teachers, and though it imposes on them a debt of gratitude, it will be a debt which shall ennoble and elevate the soul—one, which can never be canceled by gold and silver, but which demands a far richer return, even the consecration of time, talent and acquisitions to the cause of Christ."

As we know, the very concepts of right, wrong, good, evil, grandeur and degradation have been questioned and disparaged during the past century and a half, and have been largely drained of their moral force. Richard Neuhaus, in his landmark work, *The Naked Public Square,* has analyzed the moral paralysis that closes in on a society when religiously-grounded values are ruled off limits in the formal consideration of the issues that arise. Our concern here is the impact upon the individual human being of an ethos that rejects private virtue as a public good and grants supremacy to the refusal to pass judgment on individual behavior.

Let us return to that arresting comment of Brian Griffin's, "the secret knowledge that only by being good can we become joyful." I offer the hypothesis that the elusive and admirable spark within the human breast which we are examining today is only a unit of potential, which remains dormant and undeveloped until it is fertilized and animated by conscience. Spunk must be activated by a motive that subordinates the self to a larger calling. If life has no meaning beyond the fulfillment of one's own pleasures and inclinations, then there is no incentive to take the bold risks and make the sacrifices that concern us today. To activate that spirit, there must be what Duncan Williams has called the "sentiment of submission," the voluntary and ungrudging embrace of obligations to something larger and more important than the self. I would like to touch on several of the value-forming activities of our society which once served rather broadly to promulgate those ennobling obligations.

Let us begin with education. Of the innumerable analyses of the 1964 eruption at the Berkeley campus, one of the most sensitive, and perhaps most accurate, was a pair of articles by Max Ways published in *Fortune* magazine. Ways perceived that for some reason the moral energies of the students were being channeled into activities which were essentially negative, activities which complained about and attacked the structures of American society rather than working within the system in the fulfillment of moral values. He anticipated by more than two decades Allan Bloom's insight of the damaging impact of the institutionalized openness to all points of view. The emphasis placed by the academy on refusing to pass judgment on the beliefs and behavior of anyone else had served to eliminate from the educational process the approval and advocacy of standards of conduct. Virtue had somehow been redefined to be personal prejudice. Virtue had, in fact, become disreputable. There was no grandeur to be found in individual behavior. As a consequence, the only acceptable moral causes were ones to straighten out wayward institutions or force a change in wrong-headed policies. In that philosophically restricted ethical environment, almost any self-styled guru who did proclaim that he knew the way to individual glory enlisted a following larger than the validity and persuasiveness of his cause would normally deliver. In retrospect, and in the light of the understanding provided by Max Ways, this student ferment was rightly designated a protest movement. Protest is a pretty thin gruel to nourish the spirit, but for many people of that generation, that was as close as they came to moral and ethical training during their college years.

I would like to share with you a passage from a letter, which the novelist, Otis Carney, wrote several years ago about his attendance at an Ivy League college during World War II.

What I would tell [my alma mater] now is that neither she (nor any other university of our era) seemed to train us for what we were inside. There is nothing in my education that addressed itself to the "not by bread alone" part of me- the miracle of the human spirit, and by this I don't necessarily mean spirit as expressed in religion, though that is part of it. I'm talking of Pope's "know thyself." Or Eliot's "teach us to care and not to care"...When Eliot said, Teach us to care and not to care, what he seemed to be saying was: that we should care terribly about what we do in this world, hurl ourselves into it with all the intelligence and courage we can muster. And then we should not care about the reward. For, in truth, just our commitment, our energizing of our spirit in its noble connection to the struggle of all mankind—that has been our reward... Would that a student might emerge from [our university] convinced of the value of transcendence, for that is the only route to his completion.

A comparable failure on the part of the contemporary American religious institutions was brought into sharp focus by a program at Rockford College in 1973. As part of a campus-wide consideration of American Indian culture, the author/professor N. Scott Momaday spoke of the nature and practice of his Navajo faith. He told of a ceremonial song that celebrated the wonders of nature. I quote from his speech:

The singer stands at the center of sound, of motion, of life. Nothing within the whole sphere of being is inaccessible to him or lost upon him. At least we have the sense that this is so, and so does he. His song is full of reverence, of wonder and delight— and of confidence as well. He knows something about himself and the world in which he lives. And he knows that he knows. He is at peace.

At the conclusion of Dr. Momaday's speech, there was prolonged silence. Finally, there was a storm of applause. Seasoned observers knew that something extraordinary had taken place. The power of the audience response signaled much more than appreciation of a superb lecture. The speaker had struck a resonance deep within his listeners.

"Of reverence, of wonder and delight—and of confidence as well...He is at peace," said Momaday. Anyone who has worked with college students in recent years know that reverence, wonder, confidence and inner peace are rare in America's young people. Still, that infrequency doesn't necessarily signify an intentional rejection. Dr. Momaday had rendered mystery and awe and eternity, palpable and kindly, and the obligations of the participants in the Navajo faith were readily understood to be natural and benevolent, not burdens, not threats, not restrictions. And that message was warmly embraced, apparently an unfamiliar message for most of that audience.

The family, like education, religion and literature, also used to play a regular and important role in transmitting to each new generation an understanding that life requires of each person the shouldering of obligations and duties. The young learned within the home that the fulfillment of their responsibilities is not just the dues one pays for being part of a social group, but also provides both psychic and social benefits. It was the loss of this aspect of family life that Mrs. Sewall was lamenting at her 70th birthday dinner, the lapse of all those kindly, supportive, homely blessings that money can't buy. Her family had undergone a transition in which they had, as Harold Blake Walker once phrased it, "mistaken a standard of living for a purpose in life."

Among those home-bestowed blessings which money can't buy, are an unpretentious sense of self-worth and a hierarchy of values, which buttress the individual against the disappointments, and reversals of life. The Harvard research psychiatrist, Robert Coles, dwelt on the subject of suicide in a *Chicago Tribune* interview several months ago. "Many adolescent suicides we read about," he said, "make a statement about the kinds of lives these kids have been brought up to live. It is pathological narcissism at work. These kids haven't grown up with a sense that they have obligations. Acting out through suicide, is extreme self-centeredness, an attitude that has never been challenged by their parents or by their world. In fact, it may even be encouraged." Coles went on to emphasize that what leads children to self-destruction is not media attention to other youth suicides, but the "underlying festering of self-centered, unchallenged, rootless lives."

Well, what does all this add up to? This perspective is offered from one whose educational career was bisected by the watershed era of the sixties. It is difficult for today's college personnel to imagine what it was like to participate in a pre-1960 academic community when the ancient standards of lawfulness, civility, morality, truthfulness, rational debate and respect for an opposing viewpoint still carried authority and provided unity and amity within the educational enterprise. The life of the academic community, like the life of the individual human being, has been trivialized, and impoverished and rendered hollow and mean-spirited by the rejection of transcendent purpose and the cancellation of the civilized norms imposed by such purpose.

In 1956, Robert Maynard Hutchins said, "The pedagogical problem is how to use the educational system to form the kind of man that the country wants to produce. But in the absence of a clear ideal, and one that is attainable through education, the pedagogical problem is insoluble; it cannot even be stated. The loss of an intelligible ideal lies at the root of the troubles of American education." The accuracy of that analysis is certainly borne out by what has happened in the three subsequent decades. The very thought of identifying certain traits of character as desirable in all college graduates and seeking educational means to strengthen those

127

ideals of human behavior is now anathema within the reigning academic orthodoxy. Therefore, any attempt to amend the educational system to train the student for a civilized and honorable life cannot direct itself to the substance of education, but must be restricted to procedural changes, truly an exercise in rearranging the deck chairs on the Titanic. As Hutchins said, without an ideal, the problem is insoluble.

In our day, too often we continue to produce graduates who don't even have a nodding acquaintance with the visions of grandeur which shaped Western civilization, the ideals for which untold heroes and heroines of the past sacrificed that we might live in freedom today. Nor are those who did the sacrificing sufficiently known and understood to be perceived as desirable role models. The graduates of our colleges are inclined to equate pleasure with joy, because they have not been helped to learn Brian Griffin's message that only by being good can we become joyful.

It seems to me that high on the agenda for our colleges should be a plan to enlist the students as dedicated partisans of abiding, ennobling obligations.

CHAPTER XV

THE NATIONAL COUNCIL OF CHURCHES TO THE RESCUE

by
Dr. John A. Howard, President
The Rockford Institute
October 21, 1985

While the Catholic bishops have been devising a plan to rectify the economy, some Protestants have directed their remedial talents to the murky realm of television. A committee of the National Council of Churches, having completed a two-year study, has concluded that "violence in the media does lead to aggressive behavior by children, teen-agers and adults who watch the programs."

Strong measures are urged in the committee's report: the Federal Communications Commission should hold annual public hearings for producers to justify the manner in which the content of TV entertainment is determined; X- and R-rated video cassettes must not be on display in the stores that sell them; civic petitions will press the FCC to deny license renewals to stations that don't measure up; and so on—twenty-some recommendations in all.

Committee chairman, James Wall, who edits *The Christian Century*, declared that he and his colleagues are opposed to censorship, but he warned that the television industry "must clean up its act" and "avoid censorship by taking action that shows a sensitivity to the impact of violence and sexual violence, especially upon children."

The principal causes of the epidemic of television violence are identified as insufficient governmental regulation, and corporate greed, specifically, "the drive for profits far in excess of those enjoyed by the majority of American business."

If the Committee will pardon the question, "Is that so?" Although the workings of the marketplace often seem beyond the comprehension of religious bodies, it should not be too difficult to discern that there are two sides to this equation, the buyers as well as the sellers of television's wares. The buyers are numerous and enthusiastic, 98% of American homes, watching the screen on an average, according to the NCC report, of more than six hours a day.

Fortunately, what Americans do with their leisure time is still theirs to decide. If they wish to waste forty-two hours a week in non-productive videos, that is their privilege, but it does raise some questions about the institutions which are presumed to offer guidance about the purpose of life so that people may put to beneficial use the time allotted to them. It was once thought that such was the function of religion.

Moreover, if the populace favors programs which are sensational, superficial, seamy, violent and amoral, what does that say about the value-forming processes, and particularly, the religious ones designed to teach people to cherish that which is worthy and to shun that which is not. There would be little need for threats, video vigilantes and a more muscular FCC to close in on the suppliers of harmful TV fare, if the demand for it had not grown so prodigiously, fed by the moral relativism that has come to dominate the American culture.

It is to be hoped that the religious guardians of the public well-being will some day come to understand that in the free society, the virtue or the degradation of the community is the sum of the virtue or degradation of the individual citizens. The profit motive is not the villain, as many assume it to be. Among free citizens, the businessperson, like the clergyperson, teacher, doctor, carpenter or social worker, will perform honestly, amiably and charitably OR dishonestly, callously and selfishly according to the values instilled in that individual by the churches, schools, families and literature.

By any objective standard, most television entertainment is a noxious wasteland. A response to this circumstance by America's prominent religious groups is long overdue. However, this first effort, which refuses to acknowledge its own share of the blame for the problem, points the finger at non-culprits.

CHAPTER XVI

CHRISTMAS DEVOTIONAL FOR THE MEN'S CLUB

Court Street United Methodist Church, Rockford, Illinois December 13, 1982

To begin our Christmas devotional, let us turn to Matthew's brief statement of the Christmas story.

Matthew I:18-23

Now the birth of Jesus Christ was on this wise:

When as his mother Mary was espoused to Joseph, before they came together, she was found with child of the Holy Ghost.

Then Joseph her husband, being a just man, and not willing to make her a public example, was minded to put her away privily.

But while he thought on these things, behold, the angel of the Lord appeared unto him in a dream, saying, Joseph, thou son of David, fear not to take unto thee Mary thy wife: for that which is conceived in her is of the Holy Ghost.

And she shall bring forth a son, and thou shalt call his name JESUS: for he shall save his people from their sins.

Now all this was done, that it might be fulfilled which was spoken of the Lord by the prophet, saying,

"Behold, a virgin shall be with child, and shall bring forth a son, and they shall call his name Emmanuel, which being interpreted is, God with us."

133

"God with us." That was the stunning message of Christ's birth. God made himself physically known to human beings in the earthly presence of His son, a revelation which dwarfs into insignificance all other events of history. God's existence was no longer a subject of speculation. Jesus' birth brought the undeniable proof; God is with us, "Emmanuel."

This proof brought joy to the world. And it is joy I invite you to consider with me briefly this evening. Joy is an elusive concept. Joy is not the same as fun. Fun is having a good time. Joy is a glorious sense of well-being, banishing cares and pains and fears and sorrows. Joy is an impenetrable cloak of exultation which for a period of time shields us from the negative aspects of our reality.

How can we find joy? Where does joy reside? What have been the joyful moments in our own lives? For most people, one answer is found in the family context—the birth of a child or a grandchild, the sparing of a family member from a severe illness or disaster of some kind, or perhaps, Christmastime or birthdays in the family circle.

I do not think it accidental that joy is most readily associated with the family. God made the family the centerpiece of the human experience, and He made that primacy known beyond any doubt. In the instructions about how to live which God delivered to Moses on Mt. Sinai, the family was given the highest priority, the commandment to honor one's father and mother following the statement of man's obligations to God.

Furthermore, the Christmas story, itself, reaffirms the priority of the family in the divine plan of human relationships. God could just as well have delivered His son to us as a full grown, teacher and shepherd. He did not. God chose, instead, to give us the divine human presence as a baby growing up in a family. And God chose to make sure that the miraculous birth would not damage the relationship between Joseph and Mary, sending his angel to provide absolute reassurance to Joseph, who was understandably disquieted by Mary's pregnancy.

It is, therefore, not to be wondered that our recollections of joy most often are rooted in loving family relationships. And the opposite holds true, as well. Grief, in its most penetrating form, usually arises from ruptured family relationships.

As we think about our pilgrimage toward the joy of Christian living, perhaps no path will take us there more directly than the strengthening of family ties. This is not an easy course to follow, living as we do in a culture that glorifies and celebrates the individual's liberation from all obligations, especially those of pre-marital chastity, marital fidelity, the obligations of the parents to the child, and the obligations of the child to honor his father and mother. But what tragedy results from the rejection of these requirements! Recently, it was revealed that a million American children run away from home each year. "Throwaway children" they are called. Throwaway children! What a devastating critique of our society!

Perhaps the greatest gifts we can give to God in return for His transcendent gift of the Christ child to us are to breathe new strength and love into our own families and to stand tall in public life against the benighted cultural forces, which, knowing not of the role God has designated for the family, are engaged in mocking and undermining the standards of behavior which bind the loving family together.

It may be that the balance on the scales of Christian faith in any era is most clearly indicated by the relative numbers of throwaway children, for whom the family home signifies piercing grief, as contrasted with treasured children, for whom the family is a source of joy.

CHAPTER XVII

CHRISTMAS DEVOTIONAL FOR THE MEN'S CLUB

Court Street United Methodist Church, Rockford, Illinois December 14, 1989

In this season when we prepare to celebrate Christ's birth, I wish to offer as our invocation a poem by Mary Penn entitled "Second Chance."

> *Time was split in two that starry night*
> *And history fell apart;*
> *A.D. became the second chance*
> *For the kingdom of the heart*
> *The infant king God sent us*
> *Still wears his earthly crown;*
> *Throughout the world at Christmas*
> *We remember and bow down.*
> *Dear Lord, we pray this year again*
> *That all upon this earth*
> *Will celebrate with grateful hearts*
> *Our eternal Savior's birth.*

This evening I want to offer some thoughts about a passage from the gospel of St. John. These are the words of Jesus: "If ye continue in my word, *then* are ye my disciples, indeed; and ye shall know the truth and the truth shall make you free" (John 8:31,32). The audience

137

to whom he spoke was confused by what he said. They told Jesus that they had never been in bondage to anybody. How then could he make them free? Jesus replied, "Verily, I say unto you whosoever committeth sin is the prisoner of sin" (John 8:34).

The slavery Jesus had in mind was not an oppression under a governmental tyranny, nor servitude to other people. What he was saying is that people become the prisoners of their own misbehavior. The freedom he promised was freedom of the spirit. It is the profound and permanent peace of mind that comes only from having a sure and certain purpose in life and a set of instructions for achieving that purpose. Through his teachings, Jesus provided those instructions and he knew that anyone who lived by them would experience an abiding and fortifying serenity which cannot be destroyed or even diminished by any of life's circumstances. The peace of mind he promises is secure against every trouble. It is weatherproof, it is lossproof. It is even deathproof.

Let us consider as an example, one of Jesus' teachings. In the book of Matthew, Peter asked, "Lord, how oft shall my brother sin against me, and I forgive him? 'Til seven times?" Jesus replied, "I say not unto thee until seven times, but until seventy times seven" (Matthew 18: 21,22). Always forgive the other person is what Jesus tells us. In the Lord's Prayer we ask God to forgive us as we forgive those who offend us. The business of forgiving other people so we will earn God's forgiveness is sort of a tit for tat. That isn't at all what Jesus is saying. He says that our acts of genuine forgiveness are the only right thing to do and they will make our own lives better. He's right, of course. If someone has injured us or slighted us and we get angry and feel sorry for ourselves and start plotting revenge and retaliation, these are totally self-destructive sentiments. They poison our personality and sour our relationships with everyone else. A refusal to forgive does, indeed, forge a private prison for the individual. Forgiveness goes against the grain. It doesn't come easily, but once a person gets the hang of it, the world is much brighter for that person and for everyone he or she encounters.

The American society has many, many counseling services. Often these advisors tell their clients they want to help them find just the right answers for themselves, tailor made for each case. The counseling Jesus offers is of an altogether different kind. The instructions he gives apply to everyone. His intention is not to produce well-adjusted sinners. He calls on everyone to strive to be a saint. The remarkable thing is the closer we come to living by his words, the more rewarding life becomes.

Let me close with a quotation from Robert Louis Stevenson which, I think, grandly illustrates the freedom Jesus promised.

Whether any particular day shall bring to you more of happiness or suffering is largely beyond your power to determine. Whether each day of your life shall *give* happiness or suffering rests with yourself.

CHAPTER XVIII

ADDRESS TO MONDAY CLUB
OF ROCKFORD

April 3, 1988
John A. Howard

As one considers the everyday advantages we enjoy—the swift and easy transportation, the abundant, pre-packaged food, endlessly varied entertainment at the turn of an electric switch, sophisticated medical care and the other services and conveniences of modern times—the lives of our forebears of a century ago and earlier seem marvels of courage, toil and ingenuity. A stroll through the cemetery startles one with the large number of children who died at birth, or in their early years. Before the train tracks reached Rockford in 1852, it was a 24-hour trip just to reach Chicago by stage coach. The sophisticated cities of the East were a world away.

It is easy to suppose that life in the frontier towns of the Middlewest was hard and demanding and brutish, largely consumed in just meeting the requirements of survival. But that is not the way it was. The remarkable people who left New England and New York to settle this part of the land were determined that whatever deprivations their families would experience in the frontier communities, they would not be without generous spiritual and cultural nourishment. In Rockford, before the population had reached 2000 in 1850, there were already Methodist, Congregational, Baptist and Unitarian Churches. Rockford Female Seminary had been chartered and its classes begun. In 1853, the Young Men's Club was established to sponsor lectures by the leading orators of the day. Horace Mann, Horace Greeley, Ralph

141

Waldo Emerson and Henry Ward Beecher were among the notables they enlisted.

This Monday Club was one of many cultural organizations that sprang up in our town to experience, enjoy and promote literature, music, drama and art. Rare is the Midwestern town, large or small, that doesn't have 19th century homes of architectural elegance, stained glass windows and interior features of beautifully carved wood.

The impact of this determination to sustain the intellectual and aesthetic dimensions of genteel life was large and enduring. Let me report a conversation of twenty years ago. Archibald McLeish came to Rockford to give at Rockford College the first public reading of his poetical celebration of Independence Hall, entitled "The American Bell." As we drove him to his plane the next morning, he said to me, "John, I can't tell you how much I enjoyed the dinner last evening! And the people! It was an astonishing thing to me. My dinner companions were just like the finest and most cultured men and women you could meet in Boston or New York." I burst out laughing. He looked startled and, then said, "That really was awfully condescending of me, wasn't it?" "Yes," I said, "it was. Let me tell you about the second President of Rockford Female Seminary," who was, of course, his mother. "Touché!" said he. In Rockford we simply take it for granted that educated people are conversant with our cultural heritage.

When we moved to a smaller house, I began to browse through some of the books that belonged to my Grandmother and were toted from my Mother's attic after she died, to our attic and might have been conveyed directly to some attic of our family's next generation, except for this Monday Club assignment. Leafing through some of those well-worn volumes that belonged to my Grandmother Sackett, it began to dawn on me that the cultural clubs and programs and activities were not just pleasant diversions one engaged in to while away the time, and to prove to one's self, one's neighbors and the condescending Archibald McLeishes of the Eastern Seaboard that we are not untutored clods just because we live among the cow pastures and cornfields. No, those activities served a larger purpose.

Indeed, as I watched the televised representation of Lincoln's life this week, it occurred to me that possibly only the Midwest with its determined and self-conscious devotion to church and culture could have produced a leader of such insight and forbearance and fortitude as Lincoln was. Perhaps when you have heard the materials I will share with you, you will think so, too.

What follows is of a more personal nature than usually is the fare of a group presentation, so I must ask to be forgiven for admiring my Grandmother and sharing that admiration with you.

Granny Sackett was born Mary Elizabeth Manny in 1869 in the home which later became the Burpee Art Gallery. Her mother's maiden name was Florida Starr. Granny's father was John Pells Manny, who helped to develop the Water Power in Rockford, was Chairman of the committee that planned and supervised the building of the Second Congregational Church, and was engaged with his cousin, John H. Manny, in manufacturing mowers and reapers. Granny was scheduled to go East for college, against her wishes because she was in love with Charles Sackett and wanted to marry him. Somehow she fell down stairs the day before her departure, broke her leg, and married Charles Sackett a couple of months later. Among the many interests they shared was music. Both enjoyed singing and Granny was training as a concert singer.

To them was born a daughter, my mother, Edith Starr Sackett in 1890. That birth caused Granny to begin to lose her hearing and that spelled the end of her singing career. Two years later, a second daughter, Lucretia, was born, in a difficult Caesarian birth. The baby lived but two months, apparently the victim of a daily massive overdose of a tonic administered by a nurse who had misunderstood her instructions. The tragedy of that seemingly needless death was magnified when it turned out that the increasingly serious health problems for the young mother were caused by some cotton that had not been removed at the time of the Caesarian birth. We will omit further medical details other than to say that Granny was a partial invalid throughout the rest of her life unable to stand up for more than brief periods. Let's jump several decades. In the 1930's when the banks failed at about the time my grandfather retired, he and his wife not only lost the family savings which had been put into bank stock, but they were obliged to pay an additional dollar for every

143

dollar of face value of the worthless stock. They had to borrow to make the payment, but through the years they managed to pay off that debt out of grandfather's retirement pay, by living very frugally.

One might suppose that such a sequence of misfortunes would embitter an individual so victimized, but that was not the case. Granny not only rejoiced in each day, but she had a large reserve of extra joy to spread into the lives of others. For my brothers and me, the visits to Rockford were happy, almost magic, times. Granny would read to us. In preparation for our visits, she would select from *Grimm's Fairy Tales* or *The Wonder Clock* or innumerable other sources the stories best suited to the age and temperament of the child or children at hand. She also would teach us about the trees and wild flowers and birds, especially the birds.

As one who was obliged to spend much of her life lying down, she began to study birds, considering herself especially blessed because the Rock River outside her window was a major flyway for the migratory species. This little book is her bird diary for the months of February and March. Inside the front cover, she has written a little note, "Courage is fear that has said its prayers." In the back of the volume is a chart with notations for the years from 1901 through 1945 of the date in March each year when she first saw a representative of each of ninety-four different kinds of birds. I had no idea there was that rich a menu for the bird-watchers hereabouts. I won't try to relay the whole list, but, for example, the ducks she enumerates are the Baldpate, Butterball, Black, Golden-eyed, Mallard, Merganser, Pintail, Redhead, Ring-necked, Ruddy, Teal and the Greater and Lesser Scaup. The sparrows included the Chipping, Field, Fox, Henshaw, Lincoln, Savanna, Song, Swamp, Vesper and White-Throated.

Some of the birds she recorded only once or twice in the forty-four year period. In time, she became widely known as an accurate and reliable source of information about birds and the *Chicago Tribune* would occasionally ask her in the spring months what birds could be expected to be coming through Northern Illinois in the coming week or two. You can imagine the thrill she experienced when some rare bird came to her river yard and the eager excitement she communicated to her grandchildren on such occasions. No winner of the pick-six lotto grand-prize today ever felt more richly blessed than she did when one of her rare birds came by.

An avid reader, Granny could call from her memory poems, verses from the Bible, quotations from books and essays for any occasion and enjoyed writing her own little poems or doggerel for birthdays or valentines or out of sheer pleasure about something that pleased her. In her well-worn copy of Thomas A. Kempis' *Imitation of Christ* she has copied inside the front cover a passage that appealed to her. "Who am I? I am fundamentally what I love. Do I love truth? Then sooner or later I shall become true. Do I love nobility? Then ultimately, with much stumbling and faltering steps, I shall climb to the height where nobility dwells, above the strife for place and power, above low aims and self-seeking. Where your heart is, there, ultimately, you shall be also."

Her daughter, Edith, was not without prolonged adverse circumstances in her own life. Granny made for her a diary of passages of inspiration and reassurance, each page containing a quotation from the Bible and some other message of good cheer. I have selected some of my favorites from that book to share with you.

Jan. 20 Sir James M. Barrie 1860-1927 Scottish novelist, playwright. *Admirable Crichton, Peter Pan, Dear Brutus*
Those who bring sunshine to the lives of others cannot keep it from themselves.

Jan. 25 Robert Browning 1812-1889
The common problem yours, mine, everyone's
Is—not to fancy what were fair in life
Provided it could be—but, finding first
What may be, then find how to make it fair
Up to our means: a very different thing.

Jan. 27 Walter Malone 1866-1915 *Opportunity*
They do me wrong who say I come no more
When once I knock and fail to find you in:
Each morn I stand again beside your door
To bid you wake and rise and fight and win.

Weep not for precious chances passed away.
Wail not for golden ages on the wane:
Each night I burn the records of that day.
At sunrise every soul is born again.

March 21 Priscilla Leonard
"This is the lesson of the Spring:
That all things change, that all things grow,
That out of Death's most frozen woe
Come life and joy and blossoming;
That all things open and unfold
Toward the new from out the old,
Till loss has gain for following;
That Life renewing out of Death,
Onward forever traveleth
Toward its divine perfectioning—
This is the lesson of the Spring.

Feb. 11 "Shall we know in the hereafter
All the reasons that are hid?
Does the butterfly remember
What the caterpillar did?—
How he waited, toiled, and suffered
To become a chrysalid?

"When we creep so slowly upward,
When each day new burden brings,
When we strive so hard to conquer
Vexing sublunary things,
When we wait and toil and suffer
We are working for our wings."

May 25 Clarence Urmy 1858-1923 *Old Songs Are Best*
"Not what we have, but what we use;
Not what we see, but what we choose—
These are the things that mar or bless
The sum of human happiness.

"The things near by, not things afar;
Not what we seem, but what we are—
These are things that make or break,
That give the heart its joy or ache.
"Not as we take, but as we give;
Not as we pray, but as we live—
These are the things that make for peace
Both now and after time shall cease."

June 11 Ralph Waldo Emerson 1803-1882
Unitarian Minister 3 yrs. Lecturer Transcendentalist
"So nigh is grandeur to our dust,
So near is God to man,
When Duty whispers low, *Thou must*,
The youth replies, *I can*."

May 13 John Galsworthy 1867-1933 English Poet 1932 Nobel
Prize *Forsyte Saga*
    "When any one of us has seen, or heard, or read that which is
beautiful he has known an emotion precious and uplifting. A
choir boy's voice, a ship in sail, an opening flower, a town of
night, a lovely poem, leaf shadows, the stars, the crescent moon,
the thousand sights, or sounds or words, that wake in us the
thought of beauty— these are the drops of rain that keep the
human spirit from death by drought. How little savor there would
be left in life if beauty were withdrawn. It is the smile on the
earth's face, and needs but eyes to see, the mood to understand."

July 5 Ella Wheeler Wilcox 1855-1919 *Poems of Passion Poems
of Pleasure*
"'Tis easy enough to be pleasant
When life flows along like a song;
But the man worth while is the one who will smile
When everything goes dead wrong.

"For the test of the heart is trouble,

147

And it always comes with the years,
And the smile that is worth the praise of the earth
Is the smile that comes through tears."

April 13 John Bunyan 1628-1688. English Baptist Lay Preacher.
Pilgrim's Progress
    "We shall not be doomed to death or life according to the
hectoring spirits of the world, but according to the wisdom and
law of the Highest. Therefore what God says is best, indeed is
best, though all the men in the world are against it."

March 13 Thoreau 1817-1862
Of course it is the spirit in which you do a thing which makes it
interesting whether it is sweeping a room or pulling turnips.

March 18 Henry Van Dyke
All the bars at which we fret
That seem to prison and control
Are but the doors of daring set
Ajar before the soul
Say not, "Too poor," but freely give
Sigh not, "Too weak," but boldly try
You never can begin to live
Until you dare to die.

January 8 Robert Louis Stevenson British Novelist Poet Essayist
1850-1894. Life long victim of tuberculosis. *Treasure Island.*
*Child's Garden of Verses. The Strange Case of Dr. Jekyll & Mr.
Hyde.*
    The finest trait in the character of St. Paul was his readiness
to be damned for the salvation of anybody else. And surely we
should all endure a little weariness to make one face look brighter
or one hour go more pleasantly in a mixed world.

January 9
A happy man or woman is a better thing to find than a five pound
note. He or she is a radiating focus of good will. They practically

demonstrate the Great Theorem of the Livability of Life.

Mary Lyon. Founded Mt. Holyoke College.
Character, like embroidery, is made stitch by stitch.

July 1 Marcus Aurelius. Emperor of Rome 121-180.
The perfection of moral character consists in passing every day as though it were the last.

July 4 Edith Cavell. British nurse in Belgian Hospital. Shot by Germans for aid to Allied prisoners.
Standing as I do tonight in view of God and eternity, I realize that patriotism is not enough. I must have no hatred or bitterness in my heart.

It is time to close this recitation, but I have only tapped a small part of the riches in that Thought-For-The-Day-Book.

Two concluding observations—with time set aside each day to nourish the mind and heart and soul with inspiration such as this, one can appreciate how the grandmother and her daughter stood up to whatever trials and reverses life dealt them without losing their confidence in the goodness of God and with their reservoir of joy still full enough to share with everyone who came by.

The second thought—The authors that were drawn on for Granny's calendar book were not obscure writers appreciated by only a few. They were famous, broadly read and widely appreciated. It is not amiss to suppose that the culture of a century ago provided a far more civilized and humane America in which to live and raise a family. We would do well, I think, to reopen the books of that generation of inspirational authors.

CHAPTER XIX

SOME UNREMEMBERED DIMENSIONS OF LEADERSHIP

Address at Illinois Boys' State Conference
by
Dr. John A. Howard – President, Rockford College
held at Eastern Illinois University
Charleston, Illinois
June 27, 1974

Several years ago as a member of the National Commission on Marijuana and Drug Abuse, I found myself in conversation with a college student of obvious brains and talent, who was spending a prolonged term in a foreign jail for an offense having to do with illegal drugs. Understandably he regretted the part of his life that he was obliged to spend in prison, but he had recognized that since he had more time than anything else, he might as well use it to think through carefully what was really important to him in this world, so that when he was eventually released, he could utilize the rest of his life well and in fact, make up for the living time he had lost. It was a memorable experience to listen to someone of any age who had such a clear vision of what he regarded as the important things.

As our visit drew to a conclusion, I asked at what points he would focus his attention. He responded quickly more or less in these words: "I would try to convince the people in positions of leadership to accept the responsibility of their positions, to stand up and be counted on those things they consider important. For some reason, most adults seem unwilling to say flat out what their experience has taught them about the complicated business of living. Why do you people in education give your students the double talk about everyday decisions, and save your glory statements for pronouncements about Vietnam or civil rights or some other important but remote situation? Why do you leave the young to flounder around, trying to learn what is good sense and what is error by experiment or guesswork?

I have periodically thought about his comment and his question, but I haven't talked much about them because I haven't been able to figure out a very satisfactory answer. Why are people in positions of responsibility reluctant to say publicly and unselfconsciously this is what I believe, and believe with every fiber of my being? I still don't know. And I feel awkward in taking a try at it now, but, friends, here we go for better or for worse, so fasten your seat belts.

You are among the privileged few, privileged in having natural talents which have brought you to positions of importance in your schools and your communities, leading to your selection for this Boys' State conference. Like it or not, you are already leaders. I want to share with you my convictions about what is required of the true leader, the kind of leader whose life record makes everyone a little prouder to belong to the human race.

First of all, such a leader's life is characterized by integrity. Integrity certainly includes the concept of honesty. Think about it a little. If you are associated with a leader who from time to time, lies a little about what he did or why, you aren't ever really sure he is telling you the truth in matters of importance to you. He is not the kind of person you are going to follow eagerly into difficult or dangerous territory. The same thing is true with regard to the consistency with which he observes the laws and other general rules of conduct. If he decides which laws he will simply ignore—perhaps he uses pot sometimes—or if he cheats a little on an exam, the people with whom he works and the projects in which they are jointly engaged are always in jeopardy of being discredited by his dishonesty. Such a person may have some skills in organizing a project, or a high degree of personal magnetism and persuasion, but his leadership will always be founded on shaky ground. His followers will generally have to keep looking over their shoulder to see if the leader's dishonesty is about to do them in.

This much is fairly obvious. Integrity, however, is a much larger concept than just honesty. Integrity is the mark of a person who lives by a strict code of values that reflects a whole philosophy of life. Integrity is much broader than the simple observance of the constraints of truth and law. It involves conducting one's life in an honorable fashion with regard to all people—friends and strangers, allies and opponents. This dimension was brought home to me last week in a conversation with an elderly judge from Minnesota. He was talking about the difference in his working relationships with lawyers of his own generation as contrasted with the new lawyers. With the older ones, he very comfortably makes commitments over the phone, knowing that on both sides of the conversation the person's word is his bond, and no trickery is involved. With many of the younger lawyers with whom he deals, he will not register a formal reaction until after he has had the pertinent legal documents in hand and after he has studied every "Whereas" and every comma.

He was not suggesting, I believe, that the latter group was dishonest, but rather that it was cagey, withholding information or reserving a margin of commitment for negotiation later on. That way of doing things may win a few extra points for a given client, but it also makes the people with whom the person does business a little suspicious about what surprises he may have for them further down the road. The leader who possesses integrity will not engage in subterfuge in his dealings with anyone, and the dividends from his consistent forthrightness will multiply in his relationships with all people, not only those who are dependent upon him, but in his relationships, too, with those who may be his adversaries.

The second quality of a leader of commanding stature is a deep and abiding commitment to a set of ideals. Ideals are concepts of what is perfect or worthy, good or true or beautiful. Ideals have fallen onto evil times in our society. They seem to have been downgraded or shunted aside or, in the view of some people, discredited as one of the illusions of a bygone era. You just don't encounter them much any more. One of the forces which has tended to diminish the enthusiasm for ideals is the human tendency to criticize and find fault, a tendency which has been raised to the level of a national pastime. Everybody seems to be pointing the finger at somebody else, drawing attention to the other fellow's shortcomings. Indeed, some very dull people are making whole careers out of fault-finding.

One particular specialty among the enthusiasts of criticism is the systematic dismantling of the favorable image of the individuals and the social institutions which have in the past been held up as ideals. Scholars and authors have gone to some pains to proclaim the human foibles of Abraham Lincoln and Winston Churchill, of Carl Sandburg, and even Jesus Christ. Others have been very busy showing that the institution of marriage is really a mess, or that the traditional family is outmoded, that our economic system has outlived its usefulness or our form of government is no longer serviceable.

Another thrust of our times which has tended to decrease the acceptance of ideals has been the development of the so-called "New Morality" which is a formalized line of reasoning that led rather directly to the do-your-own-thing philosophy. Oscar Wilde once observed that the best way to get rid of temptation is to give in to it. One can cite a whole litany of clichés which justify practically anything: One man's heaven is another man's hell, beauty is in the eye of the beholder, there are no eternal values, and so forth.

Well, let me suggest that the human being is not perfect and it is rather unlikely that he will become so. All human institutions, therefore, are forever destined to be imperfect because their designers are human, as are the people responsible for making them operate, so nobody should be very much surprised if anyone who enjoys being critical and tearing things down finds a wart here and there on the face of our heroes, or a squeaky cog in some of the social machinery which has been constructed by toil and sacrifice through the ages. But how foolish we would be if we let the petty people who engage in their little fault-finding take away from us the ideals toward which we would reach and stretch, albeit haltingly!

We must not let anyone shatter the image of an Abraham Lincoln as a true and noble example of humility and of the generous heart, or the true image of a Churchill as an inspiring example of courage responding to the threat of tyranny, when courage was about the only weapon which Churchill and his countrymen had at hand with which to respond. A man's reach must exceed his grasp or life is without progression. The most effective leader has a very clear vision of the ideals toward which he and his associates are striving, and the fact that they will never altogether achieve those ideals but can only move toward them, in no way invalidates the unifying and motive power which those ideals provide to that group.

Along with integrity and ideals, the third asset of the capable leader I want to pose for your consideration is inspiration. Mr. Robert Galvin, Chairman of the Board of Motorola, speaking to a group of college presidents some years ago, asserted that perhaps the greatest requirement of a chief executive is to spread hope. The intervening years have served to underscore the wisdom of that thought. If there is anything which people need today more than anything else, it is hope. There seems to be a widespread uneasy suspicion that mankind may not be smart enough to solve the problems that have arisen.

To the extent that people are feeling such an uneasiness, I suspect we are seeing the consequences of the new illiteracy. Our citizens can put the letters together and read the words, but too seldom does our education provide the student with a useful comprehension of historical perspective. Anyone who has studied and registered upon the flow of history knows that life has never been easy. It is only in recent years that people have become so affluent and so arrogant as to suppose that life can be easy or should be easy. The Black Death wiped out a quarter of the population of Europe in the 1300's. The potato crop failure in Ireland in 1845 and 1846 literally eliminated the principal source of food for a nation. Through most of Western history, one powerful tyrant or another was trying to capture the civilized world. In our own country, the first meager settlements were scratched out of a wilderness. During the Civil War, there were 53,000 casualties at the Battle of Gettysburg in just three days.

Well, in this critical business of spreading hope, I believe that that leader will be most successful who is equipped with a working knowledge of history so that he is mindful of the wars and pestilence and famine and cataclysms, but also, and much more important, he

155

has fixed in his understanding the stories of heroism and sacrifice and human dignity in the face of adversity. Winston Churchill is, of course, one supreme example of the leadership capacity that is strengthened by being steeped in a vast reach of historical lore.

To Mr. Galvin's precept of spreading hope, I would add one I consider of equal importance, spreading joy. If the people who are working together have a good time doing so, the limits of what that particular group can accomplish are greatly extended. There are, of course, some favored individuals who seem to be happy by nature and have an easy gift for spreading their good cheer wherever they go. They don't seem to need any help in providing inspiration in the joy department. For the rest of us, some help is needed.

Many years ago, I chanced to become acquainted with an elderly scientist who, although he had been retired for a long time, was possessed of one of the liveliest and best informed minds I have ever encountered. He also carried with him an aura of cheerfulness and serenity that marked him as a very extraordinary human being. One day I asked him how he managed to remain so calm and so cheery in a world that seemed so combative and so confused. He replied that it was his friends who sustained his good spirits, and with a gesture he indicated that his "friends" were the books with which he had surrounded himself.

"You know, John", he said, "from time to time I have encountered a book or an article or a quotation which spoke very directly to me in a positive way, an anecdote, an analysis or a poem which had an inspirational or a regenerative influence, or which was the distillate of some basic bit of wisdom. These I have kept and ranged on the shelves according to the particular tonic which they offered to me, much as the pharmacist organizes his remedies according to the malady to be treated. There is no piece of news so depressing, no individual loss so debilitating, no personal success so inflating but what I have here half a dozen literary medications to set it right."

Let me suggest a few prescriptions which I have found helpful when the pulse of joy has been at low ebb. On the first shelf of this manuscript medicine cabinet, one might put the master satirists who know precisely how to put into perspective those people who get puffed up with their own importance. The mockery of a short column by Art Buchwald can more devastatingly deflate a pretentious demagogue than a solid month of well- reasoned arguments on "Meet The Press". Some of Buchwald's brightest gems are just as refreshing years after the event as they were the day they were printed. Lawrence Durell's anecdotes about Britain's terribly proper elite Foreign Service officers as they encountered bizarre situations could, I imagine, lift the most depressed mope out of his doldrums, particularly his essays in the volume entitled *Esprit de Corps*. P. G. Wodehouse is another deflator of rare and apparently eternal talent.

But the grand master of them all, I believe, was William S. Gilbert of the Gilbert & Sullivan operetta team. His librettos are characterized by a consummate skill in gently unmasking that which is pompous, ponderous, or spurious. Indeed, when he poked fun at Queen Victoria, that hallowed institution who ruled Britain for almost two-thirds of a century, she departed from the regal stance of ignoring the barbs of a mere playwright, and cast about for some means of retaliation. Ultimately, the best she could do was to knight his partner, Arthur Sullivan, leaving him a mere commoner. The range of Gilbert's subjects for satire comprises a minor lexicon of human foibles, a rich reservoir for the writer or public servant to draw upon when his own powers of perception or expression fall short. If only we had a Gilbert & Sullivan today to teach us to laugh at ourselves a little, we could, I think, better survive this period of earnest and ponderous agony in our nation's government.

A second shelf in my cabinet of prescriptions for joy would house some of the simple and forthright stories of families that had the integrity and the courage and the affectionate cohesiveness to meet and surmount effectively the obstacles, small and large, which life always seems to interpose between birth and death.

Of all the authors who have documented lives lived with dignity and confidence, my favorite is Ralph Moody, whose autobiographical novels tell the story of homesteading in Colorado on a ranch with an inadequate water supply. They can be read merely as delightful, entertaining and fast-moving tales of frontier life, but they are much, much more than that. They present the high drama of principle confronting the problems of everyday living. They illustrate the raw material out of which a person can weave the fabric of joy into his life. If you haven't read *Little Britches* and its sequel, *Man of The Family*, give yourself a treat, and I suspect you will be reading them aloud to your own children not too many years hence. These are a few samples of what I have found to be useful antidotes for gloom.

Dr. Frost's formula for good cheer is a simple one, but not often utilized. Each of us comes across literary works which speak personally to us in an affirmative way, which bring warm light into our day. Any work that can do that is worth re-reading. If we will just collect these items and turn to them in time of need, we can cut way down on the psychiatrist's bills and what is more, by our own improved spirits, make life a little pleasanter for those around us. Dr. Frost's technique can, I believe, put joy "on reserve" for that person who will actually use the literary prescriptions which he has assembled.

Well, these are some thoughts I would share with young leaders if ever I were invited to do so. Integrity, ideals, and inspiration are, I believe, three "eyes" that extend the vision of any person and which, when cultivated and implemented, can give a leader a genuine and wholesome power that will tend to make his projects prosper far beyond those which are not animated by these guiding principles.

CHAPTER XX

COMMENCEMENT ADDRESS AT ROCKFORD COLLEGE

May 15, 1994
By Dr. John A. Howard
Counselor, The Rockford Institute
(Former President of Rockford College)

Bob Hope, I am told, once began a commencement address in this manner: "It is a frightful responsibility to have to figure out what to say to young people as they complete their studies and move out into a confused and belligerent world. After much agonizing, I finally hit on a good thought. My advice to you as you prepare to go from this campus and face the turmoil and tribulations of life is, Don't go!"

Fifty years ago today, I too, was facing a kind of graduation day. I was more than a little uneasy about what would happen afterwards. I was in England, with many other Americans, finishing our military training for the invasion of Normandy. As the days dwindle down before the first encounter with enemy fire, many thoughts rattle around in one's head. You wonder if you can handle it. If you will do what you are counted on to do when bullets and bombs are coming your way. You wonder which people around you will keep their cool when the going gets rough. You wonder if the antagonism among a few people in your unit will prevent them from the instant cooperation that combat demands.

As it turned out such nervous conjectures were a waste of time. Although I didn't recognize or understand it until long after the war ended, the uniquely important aspect of human character that made combat bearable and caused most soldiers to perform well under fire was a quality of human nature that hasn't had much attention. From observation in eleven months of combat and over the years that followed, it seems clear to me that every person is capable of experiencing deep satisfaction from helping someone else. The act of helpfulness strengthens the helper.

You will recall in First Corinthians (XIII. 13) Paul concludes his tribute to charity with these words, "And now abideth faith, hope and charity, and the greatest of these is charity." Charity, that divine spark of helpfulness, lies deep beneath all the automatic first tendencies toward self-preservation, self- interest and self-indulgence. Some people live their whole lives without ever discovering or activating their charitable impulse. That is a great misfortune, for the life lived only at the level of self-interest is unfulfilled, deprived of the abiding satisfactions and joys that come from being helpful.

Well friends, joys and satisfactions are rather scarce items in warfare, but the ones generated by helpfulness are always available. They cannot be blocked or diminished by war or poverty or sickness or any other adverse situation. A person can always choose to focus on what will benefit someone else. In combat the acts of helpfulness became a way of life for many soldiers, creating a self-replenishing source of courage and morale. Helpfulness proved a shield against the fears and tensions of wartime. It was the seedbed in which heroism is formed and nourished.

One of the great heroes of our century came to Rockford College some years ago. His name is Abba Eban. He was born in South Africa and educated in England. He served in the British Army. After the nation of Israel was created, he migrated there and had become that country's foreign minister when a crisis occurred in 1967. The Egyptian dictator, Gamel Abdul Nasser, seeking revenge against Israel for an earlier military humiliation, expelled the United Nations' peace-keeping forces from the Gaza Strip and blockaded Elat, Israel's only port on the Red Sea.

It was a moment of frightening tension in the world, with explosive ramifications in the Cold War. Nasser's hostile actions precipitated what became known as the Six-Day War. Abba Eban went to the United Nations and, in a televised speech, accused the Soviet Union of being the instigator and clandestine partner in Egypt's provocations. It was a challenge of breath-taking candor and courage and forcefulness. I doubt if there has ever been a more anxious and astonishing drama at the United Nations than that accusation.

From that moment I began sending invitations to Mr. Eban to speak at Rockford College. After several years he was able to accept. For forty-five minutes he spoke without a note about Israel and the international situation. The extraordinary impact of his speech was, in part, due to the lucid analysis of critical matters and the Churchillian English in which he expressed himself, but also to the keen awareness throughout the audience that there wasn't an ounce of self-importance in the man. His devotion to the nation and the principles he served was all-encompassing.

I want to provide a footnote here about why Rockford College will always be as unforgettable to Mr. Eban as the clarity and power of his address were to each person who heard him. It was a warm day and the gymnasium was crowded. When his speech was concluded, he sat down heavily in the large elegant armchair we had brought from Forrest Cool Lounge. The chair had casters on it and rolled backward on the platform until it hit a little retainer board. Then the chair tipped over. The huge hanging Rockford College banner gave way as Mr. Eban disappeared from sight. I thought, "Migosh! We've killed one of the world's greatest statesmen!" Fortunately, he was not badly damaged.

One other item out of Rockford College's past deserves comment in this sequence. When I came to Rockford College on February 1, 1960, this campus acreage was just woods and cornfields. The property had been procured several decades earlier through the farsightedness, persistence and persuasiveness of one person, Blanche Walker Burpee. She anticipated that the riverside location where the college was originally built would one day be inadequate. The Great Depression forestalled any possibility of an early relocation, but Mrs. Burpee was able to convince enough people of the long-term need for a new campus that they bought shares and held this property in trust until another generation of college people was able to fulfill her dream.

The first buildings were occupied in 1961. And for three years the men lived on the new campus, the women lived on the old campus. Morning classes were downtown; afternoon classes were on East State Street. In those years, Rockford College had a split personality. The logistics of commuting and the challenge of sustaining a unified morale were about as difficult as was the need to find new gifts to pay for the enormous and ever-growing costs of construction.

By the summer of 1964 enough buildings were completed on the new campus to permit the consolidation of everything and everybody in the wonderful new quarters. But there was a huge problem. There wasn't any money available for the cost of moving. The business manager, Jack Heckinger, said, "We'll just do it ourselves with volunteer labor and borrowed trucks." I said, "Jack, are you out of your mind? Moving the library collection alone is out of the question. Have you ever packed and moved just one household's worth of books?" "We can do it", he said.

On August 15, 1964 at 7:30 a.m., more than 100 volunteers—students, alumni, faculty, boy scouts, and many others—assembled in the downtown College Chapel to get their work assignments and instructions. 12 Rockford trucking companies donated 16 large vans for the day and innumerable smaller trucks of every size and shape were used to transport 5000 cartons, chairs, desks, beds, dressers, lab equipment, etc.... Every item was marked with its destination as to building and room. The Red Cross supplied first aid stations at both ends of the journey. Alumni provided a 9:30 coffee break and a farm-sized luncheon. The task was completed by mid-afternoon. The only dollar cost was for the repair of the frame of a small borrowed truck that had buckled under the weight of library books.

Even more remarkable than the successful completion of a gargantuan labor was the exhilaration of the laborers. The move was a drama of good will and self-restoring energy and unwavering cheerfulness that amalgamated a heterogeneous group of workers into a highly effective labor force.

Whereas skillfully applied logistics and unusual physical exertion would hardly be expected to culminate in one of the peaks of history for an academic institution, the move did, I believe, constitute such an event for Rockford College.

A service organization rises to heights or remains insignificant according to the character of its personnel. A service organization is sabotaged by egotism, pomposity, jealousy or self-righteousness. The move was an inspirational event for it was a consummate demonstration of single-minded service with each participant, regardless of strength, age or calling, doing the utmost to complete whatever needed next to be done.

What do these little glimpses of past events have in common? Why were these items chosen? Because in each instance, there is an extraordinary and admirable result that comes from subordinating a concern for one's self to a worthy endeavor. The mutual helpfulness of the soldiers in combat, Abba Eban's single-minded dedication to his nation's well-being, the cheerful and unflagging persistence of Mrs. Burpee in acquiring the new campus and the heroic labors of the volunteer brigade that transported the college's materiel to East State Street—all are instances of the public and personal benefit of what Duncan Williams called the "Sentiment of Submission", that is the giving of oneself in service.

The Roman Catholic Church still uses the term "vocation" to describe a God-given commitment to devote one's life to the church. Actually, the word "vocation" means a calling. Both calling and vocation are terms that used to signify the life-work of every individual. They implied a sense of mission, of service, not just a matter of earning one's living. Those who succeed greatly in anything, whether it is paid work, or parenting or providing a new campus, are those who address themselves with a deep and abiding sense of vocation.

Finally, one of the great advantages of attending Rockford College, as I have tried to suggest, is that the experience here is enriched far beyond the substance of classroom learning, for that classroom learning can be applied within a broad understanding of God and mankind that is absorbed from encountering on this campus people who benefit the world through their selfless service.

May God bless each of you graduates in the years ahead.

CHAPTER XXI

AMERICA'S QUIET GIFT TO THE OTHER PEOPLES SERVICE ABOVE SELF

Address by John A. Howard, Counselor,
The Rockford Institute
Delivered at the Installation of Dr. Ray Den Adel as
Governor of Rotary International District #6420,
Rockford, Illinois, June 27, 1997

Honored Guests, Rotarians, Friends of Rotary: We have assembled to launch a dauntless Classics scholar on a strenuous year-long Odyssey. We are here to congratulate him on his selection as a District Governor of Rotary International and to praise and thank him for accepting this arduous responsibility, which requires visiting and speaking in many communities. In effect, he will be taking his classroom on the road for twelve months.

What is it that can justify such a substantial redirection of his life and of the lives of 520 other district governors throughout the world?

Well, the saga of Rotary is an astonishing one. Consider just a few facts. The Rotary club was founded in America in 1905. There are now 28,000 Rotary clubs in 155 countries. 67,000 new members were enlisted last year. Over the years, Rotarians have donated $320,000,000 for 30,000 scholarships. Rotary has mounted a worldwide campaign against polio which has already immunized one billion children. Every one of the 28,000 clubs benefits its own community with a variety of helpful programs. What is the magic of this organization? What is the motive force that has enabled Rotary to work these wonders? It is the answer to that question I wish to dwell on this evening.

Let us begin with a little story. Back in the Middle Ages a British Knight was returning to the castle one evening after a long, hard day of skirmishes. His armor was dented, his helmet was askew, and most its plume was broken off, his horse was limping and he was listing to one side on the saddle. The Lord of the manor saw him coming and went out to greet him, "You look terrible! What hath befallen you, Sir Albert?" he asked.

The Knight straightened himself up and said, "Oh, Sire, I have been striving in your behalf all day, robbing and pillaging and burning the towns of your enemies to the west."

"You've been doing what?" asked the astonished nobleman. The Knight repeated his statement louder and slower in case the fellow couldn't hear well.

"But I haven't any enemies to the west," cried the nobleman.

"Oh!" said the Knight. Then after a pause, "Well, I think you do now."

There is a moral to this story, friends. Enthusiasm is not enough. You have to have a sense of direction. You need to understand not only what you are doing, but why. Rotary has a compass that provides direction for all its activities and for the lives of its members. It is a model of clarity and simplicity, a three-word directive- Service Above Self.

At Rotary's first convention in 1910, this objective was phrased, "He profits most who serves his fellows best." Over the years, several refinements of this motto eventually led to the present version. That "He profits most" phrase from the early times bears some thought. In the context of an association formed originally by business and professional men, one may suppose that the profit they had in mind was increased dollar gain. But making Rotarians wealthier is not what that slogan is all about. Service above self is a formula for activating an element of human nature that brings to the individual satisfactions for greater than monetary rewards.

This phenomenon is apparent in the sheer joy of the small child as he gives to his mother a picture he has drawn in kindergarten. It is the "giving" that delights the little kid. Service above self restores the soul. It provides remedy and protection for mental and emotional stress. I want to illustrate the point with another true story from World War II. The Allies had advanced to the Rhine River when just before Christmas, the Nazis mounted a bold and desperate counterattack which came to be know as the Battle of the Bulge. The tank battalion in which I served found itself on the north flank of the Nazi drive. We were in a small town in Belgium through which ran one of the few good roads to the industrial cities of the north. Our mission was to repel any enemy efforts to move northward along that road.

The tide of war had taken the Allies beyond the town into Germany several weeks before and the civilians who had survived in their basements or in the neighboring woods were trying to put together some pieces of their daily life when the war returned and their community once again became a battleground. On Christmas morning as we waited for the next attack, the armor of our tanks sheltered us from the shrapnel of the artillery fire. We were therefore amazed to see a girl, who could not have been more than eight or nine years old, hurry from a nearby house to the side of our tank. She asked if we had any food to spare. She told us her mother had taken the younger children to another town, but she stayed behind to care for her grandfather who had been wounded and couldn't travel. The tank crew, with no hesitation gave her the rations that were in the tank. She said, "Thank you! Thank you! It is a lovely Christmas after all." And away she ran, her arms full of the ugly, brown, heavily-waxed boxes of k-rations.

The truly remarkable thing was that the soldiers who gave up their food also felt it was a lovely Christmas after all. These men, who for weeks had been living outside in cold and snow, who had had little sleep and had been under immanent threat of death for days and nights, were powerfully restored by a simple act of generosity. Service above self, acts of kindness, constitute a universal language that transcends adversity, that crosses any frontier, that speaks without an interpreter to any nation. It is a language the deaf can hear and the blind can read. It knits humanity together in a very positive way.

Human beings do not have a very good record of being able to live together in peace and friendship. The daily news offers a regular outpouring of struggle and conflict and cruelty throughout the world. One wag has suggested that if anyone who follows the news is not in a perpetual state of fear and depression, he needs to have his television set fixed.

The United States government has been sending troops and diplomatic missions to Haiti and Bosnia and the Middle East and the Far East and Africa to try to diminish the hatreds and strife and bloodshed. The intentions have undoubtedly been benevolent. The results are at best disappointing.

By contrast, Rotary International serves as an international healing and binding force of immense power. Rotary has innumerable programs of international service, each with its own inspirational record of helpfulness and friendships and accomplishments that move forward and gather momentum uninhibited by national boundaries or ancient hostilities.

Listen to this excerpt from the April issue of the *Rotarian*:

> The struggle to achieve polio eradication is a public-health story of epic proportions, unprecedented in terms of international cooperation, public/private teamwork, voluntary donations and personal sacrifice...
>
> Rotarians have helped lead the way by committing nearly $400 million in private funds to provide polio vaccine, technical support, medical personnel, laboratory equipment and educational materials for health workers and parents.
>
> But even more important, Rotarians have generously offered their compassion, time and expertise...
>
> In India Rotarians recruited 150,000 volunteers to support that country's first National Immunization Day in 1995. This year, Rotarians helped 2.6 million health workers and volunteers vaccinate 117 million children.

Just think about those figures for a minute. 150,000 volunteers mobilized and 117 million children immunized!! And that's just in one country. President Clinton and a host of eminent dignitaries recently mounted a heavily publicized summons to volunteerism. How much more convincing that effort would have been if they had reported on the incredible accomplishments of Rotary and the human impulse responsible for its success!!

As you know, this is the 50th anniversary of the Marshall Plan. That outpouring of American generosity to the devastated nations of Europe was unprecedented in its magnitude and in its inclusion of defeated enemies. It is a landmark assured of a place in the history books. Even so, its importance recedes in the minds of successive generations of students. The Marshall Plan's prominence in history's landscape will continue to subside over time.

By contrast, the distinguishing feature of the Rotary Club movement is seldom, if ever, mentioned in news reports or media commentaries, but it has a power and a permanence that will go on producing greater and greater benefits regardless of whether historians or news people are even aware of it.

This is, indeed, a quiet gift that Americans, by generating the Rotary Club, have given to other peoples. However, Rotary's impact is needed just as much here, and is just as beneficial here, as anywhere else. As one who spent twenty-four years as a teacher and administrator at American colleges, I have been concerned about the growing proportion of our nation's young people whose plans and aspirations give no thought to service above self.

When I was a member of the National Commission on Marijuana and Drug Abuse, one of my assignments was to visit university campuses and meet with students significantly involved in the use of illegal mind-altering drugs. I had an affidavit from the United States Attorney General stating they could talk freely to me without any legal repercussions for themselves. These were bright and sensitive people, but in many cases they felt no obligation to their parents, to the college they attended, to the country they lived in or to the laws of the land. Nothing was especially good or worth sacrificing for. Why not live it up and have some of everything?

Those young people had never been effectively introduced to the ideals of their own society. They were not guided by any concept of the good life that transcended one's own pleasures and desires. They were living in moral poverty. That experience of the Drug

169

Commission was twenty-five years ago. Things haven't gotten any better since. I want to quote now from an article Leon Wieseltier wrote several months ago in *The New Republic*. He was commenting on the suicides of the Heaven's Gate UFO cult.

> The mansion of death in San Diego made one melancholy for many reasons, and one of them was...the crudity of their vision. They had mistaken the junk of the entertainment industry for the stuff of holy life. "We watch a lot of 'Star Trek,' a lot of *Star Wars*," said one of the shaven talking heads on the tape they left behind, and "it's time to put into practice what we've learned..."
> "I've been on this planet for thirty-one years," one woman told the Camera, "and there's nothing here for me."

Of course the drug-users in 1972 and the suicidal cult of today represent the fringes of society, but the problem of the absence of "the stuff of holy life" is pervasive. There is precious little in contemporary culture—the movies, the books, the TV, the music, the classroom teaching—that touches on human grandeur, that provides inspirational guidance for living a life.

In this modern moral wasteland, Rotary International has a number of programs that serve young people in all countries that can open their understanding and their lives to the benefits of a larger, much more satisfying purpose in life, the life of service. And that transmission of a higher awareness results as much from contact with the Rotarians who live by their motto as from the substance of the Rotary youth programs.

This point brings us back to this evening's honored guest. Dr. Ray Den Adel is the embodiment of the Rotary motto. In every aspect of his personal life and professional career he has contributed far beyond the call of duty. He will be an inspirational model of, and a cheerful and articulate spokesman for Service Above Self.

CHAPTER XXII

THE DAZZLING LIGHT
FROM THE NORTH

Opening Convocation Address at
Rockford College, Rockford, Illinois
by
Dr. John A. Howard, President
September 15, 1976

"By his very existence, (he) confers moral worth upon the world he lives in... by his faith he moves mountains."[14]

These are the comments of Bernard Levin of *The* (London) *Times*. George Meany, referring to the same person, declared, "We heed this voice, not because it speaks for the left or right or for any faction, but because it hurls truth and courage into the teeth of total power."[15] Political scientist Gerhart Niemeyer has said his "appearance is one of those watershed historical events like the

---

[14] Bernard Levin, "Solzhenitsyn: Poison Darts From Among The Pygmies," *The* (London) *Times*, July 17, 1975.

[15] Solzhenitsyn: *The Voice of Freedom*, AFL-CIO Publication #152, (Undated), p. 1, Washington, D.C.

French Revolution."[16] A reviewer in the official Soviet press wrote, "But why is it upon reading this remarkable story not only is one's heart wrung with grief, but a light penetrates one's soul? It is because of the story's profound humanity."[17]

The author who evokes this extraordinary praise from such diverse commentators is, of course, Alexander Solzhenitsyn. His individual creative acts will, I believe, have a more profound and lasting impact on mankind than the works of any other individual of our age. I suggest, therefore, at the outset of our year-long study of "The Creative Process," we look to this unique talent as a basepoint for deliberating the theme we have chosen.

Let us begin with a recognition that creativity is one of the glamorous catchwords of the day. There appears to be a widespread notion that the mere creation of something is automatically a beneficial act. A moment's reflection will identify that supposition as pure nonsense. It is possible to create chains as well as chapels. It is possible to create fear as well as frescoes, bestiality as well as bridges. *If civilization is to prevail, any act of creating must ultimately be judged according to the substance and the impact of that which is created.* To be sure, the technique utilized in the accomplishment may inspire admiration, but if the outcome is human degradation, that, too, is important, whether one is judging a work of art, an act of government, a decision of a business enterprise, or the deed of an individual.

The moral consequence of human actions is a primary concern of Solzhenitsyn's work. *Candle in the Wind* is the title of a play he wrote in 1960. The plot is centered in the work of scientists in the field of biocybernetics or "biofeedback" as it is popularly known today. The protagonist of the play, Alex, is not sure it is wise to tamper mechanically with the human personality, uneasy lest the

---

[16] Gerhart Niemeyer, "Solzhenitsyn's Three Achievements," *The Intercollegiate Review,* Fall, 1975, p.3.

[17] Gerhart Niemeyer, "The Prophetic Calling of Solzhenitsyn," *National Review,* March 15, 1974, p. 320

state of happiness that is artificially induced will dehumanize the patient. In one of the interchanges between Alex and the self-confident director of the biocybernetics laboratory, Alex comments, "You once said you feel like a relay runner, that you would be proud to pass on the baton of Great Physics to the twenty-first century...Well, I'd like to help pass on to the next century one particular baton—the flickering candle of our soul."[18]

Passing that baton is Solzhenitsyn's own mission in this world. He is acutely aware that the person who seeks personal advantage at the expense of others, in addition to whatever public damage he may inflict, impoverishes his own life at its very foundation. In the play, a senior scientist, who had been riding the crest of fame and fortune on the frontiers of technological experiment, begins to put his life into perspective as death approaches. Ruefully he says to his daughter, "I've lived in this evil den of happy people and it has swallowed me up...That's how my life's been wasted, the life everyone calls a happy one."[19]

The obligation of the conscientious person to consider the consequences of his acts is a recurrent topic in Solzhenitsyn's public commentary, as well as in his literary works. In various interviews, he laments the tendency of reporters and critics to be more concerned about attracting attention to what they write than about the precision of their statements. At the Stockholm press conference when he received his Nobel Prize, one reporter queried, "In your opinion, Western-style democracy is not suitable to Russia. Why not?" Solzhenitsyn responded, "This, gentlemen, is a perfect example of how hastily and superficially the press oversimplifies people's views. Today, when we touch on serious questions, I would particularly like to request that if you are not able to report

---

[18] Alexander Solzhenitsyn, "Candle In The Wind" (excerpts), *Intellectual Digest,* January, 1974, p. 32.

[19] Ibid., p. 31.

accurately and fully, you should say nothing at all."[20]

On another occasion he notes, "Whilst enjoying such great freedom, the journalists and writers lose their sense of responsibility before history, before their own people...The press does not feel responsibility for its judgments and sticks on labels with the greatest of ease. Mediocre journalists simply make headlines of their conclusions which suddenly become the general opinion throughout the West."[21]

His distress about thoughtless and irresponsible conduct is expressed with even-handed regret and candor whether the object of his criticism is Communist or Westerner, scientist, journalist, educator or corporate executive. In a speech sponsored by the AFL-CIO, he called attention to certain American businessmen who brought to Moscow a display of their products— sophisticated equipment for crime detection. "The problem being," as William Buckley wryly observed, "that we were selling our scientific paraphernalia not to the law-abiding for use against criminals, but to criminals for use against the law-abiding."[22] Solzhenitsyn's own comment was, "This is something which is almost incomprehensible to the human mind: that burning greed for profit which goes beyond all reason, all self-control, all conscience, only to get money."[23]

Solzhenitsyn is the voice of conscience. Without condescension, but firmly and forthrightly, he applies his immense powers of perception and dramatic expression to challenge people everywhere

---

[20] Alexander Solzhenitsyn, "Solzhenitsyn Speaks Out," *National Review,* June 6, 1975, p. 605.

[21] "The Vision of Solzhenitsyn," *Firing Line,* March 27, 1976, pp. 2-3, Southern Educational Communications Association- Columbia, S.C.

[22] William F. Buckley, Jr., "Editor's Note," *National Review,* p. 929.

[23] *Solzhenitsyn: The Voice of Freedom,* AFL-CIO Publication #152, (undated) p. 5, Washington, D.C.

to anticipate the consequences of their acts and accept responsibility for those consequences. His message is particularly poignant in our era when the distinction between right and wrong has been twisted and obscured by passion, avarice, cynicism and scorn. His own life story is the triumphant proof that no matter how intently individuals and nations may try to deceive themselves with the assertion that virtue has no meaning, nevertheless the force of moral righteousness cannot be suppressed. Imagine! A provincial schoolteacher and writer whose words achieved such world impact that the most ruthless tyranny of modern times was equally afraid to kill him or to permit him to remain in the country.

In the Swiss magazine, *Impact,* literary critic Jean Dutourd wrote:

> The mark of a great writer, that which distinguishes him from a good writer or a talented man, is the burning and tireless search for truth to which he devotes his life. Truth about people, about society, about the world. Nothing is more dangerous.
>
> Why? Because a man who sees the truth and proclaims it has but one objective: to be of benefit to other people, to free them, to identify for them that which is wrong and prevent them from embracing it. But that is what people can least tolerate...
>
> Voltaire, in a burst of gallantry, once wrote to Catherine II of Russia..."in this era, it is from the North that we receive our guiding light"...It seems to me that Solzhenitsyn genuinely deserves such homage. But who in the West truly dares to look up to that dazzling guiding light?[24]

I imagine George Meany was referring to Soviet Russia when he spoke of Solzhenitsyn's "hurling truth and courage in the teeth of total power," but as Monsieur Dutourd has so bluntly stated, Solzhenitsyn's truth and courage have been hurled into the teeth of total power in the West as well. And his message of virtue is about

---

[24] Jean Dutourd, "La Lumiere Qui Vent Du Nord," *Impact,* Fevrier, 1976, p. 12. (Translation by John A. Howard).

as welcome in the decadent West as it is in the despotic East. Will Americans draw from this source of light only those selected beams which comfortably illuminate each individual's prejudices, or are there those who dare to receive and welcome his comprehensive, compelling clarification of the moral imperative?

That question has some perplexing aspects for an academic institution since respect for the open mind is a cherished and esteemed tradition, and one that has operated to discourage judgments that anything is good or bad. Solzhenitsyn, I suggest, shows us the way to honor that tradition without becoming an ally of either amorality or zealotry. He has not issued a comprehensive encyclopedia of "do's" and "don'ts." He recognizes that there are many issues where what is true and right and good is not yet clear. He does move to criticize the cheap, the dishonest and the destructive where the evidence seems conclusive, but in matters that are in doubt he focuses his concern on the questions that must be answered. In *Candle In The Wind,* Alex phrases his uneasiness about their experiments as a query. "Every time I go out of my house, I always know where I'm going and why. When I buy anything, I know why. But when it comes to an important action, it's considered for some reason that you don't need to know or think about it...Why are we doing all this? No one is able to give me an answer."[25]

Since our liberal arts studies aspire to contribute to responsible and civilized living, it seems to me that we could not do better than heed the unique and inexorable challenge which Solzhenitsyn has issued to all thinking people. What are the actual consequences of one's actions? Is the thing which is said or written, painted, or accomplished, is that thing adding dignity to human living? Is it a step further along the path of spiritual improvement? Or is it contributing to confusion, despair or degradation?

This question, I suggest, not only constitutes a proper context for our study in the abstract of "The Creative Process," but is equally

---

[25] Alexander Solzhenitsyn, "Candle In The Wind" (excerpts), *Intellectual Digest,* January, 1974, p. 30.

appropriate as the context for evaluating the specific creative process in which we are all joined, that is, the refinement and strengthening of this college. If that question could somehow become the automatic yardstick for measuring our individual and group decisions, then our college, which has already earned some small reputation in the quest for humane and civilized living, will continue to add to its candlepower as a source of enlightenment.

In conclusion, let us return to the critic with whose quotation we began this discourse, Bernard Levin of *The* (London) *Times.*

So what can we do with Solzhenitsyn? Well, if I may conclude with a modest proposal, I suggest that the West, when he has provoked it a little further, should, possibly under the auspices of the United Nations General Assembly, formally condemn him to death and execute him either by obliging him to drink hemlock or by crucifixion. After all, the two most noted figures in history who respectively experienced those fates were condemned, whatever the ideological niceties involved, principally because they told their own societies truths that made those societies uncomfortable, and since our own society is even more averse to discomfort than those were, it seems only fitting that the man who is...doing much the same thing for us should suffer a like fate. Meanwhile, I can look at the hand that shook the hand of the man who shook the world and say to him, "Aleksandr Isayevitch, do not despair just yet, we understand."[26]

My hope for the year ahead is that we, too, can say, "we understand," and strive to deliver on that understanding.

---

[26] "The Vision of Solzhenitsyn," *Firing Line,* March 27, 1976, p. 1. Southern Educational Communications Association- Columbia, S.C.

CHAPTER XXIII

GAY RIGHTS IN A LARGER PERSPECTIVE

John A. Howard, Senior Fellow
The Howard Center for Family,
Religion and Society
September 20, 2000

The gay rights agenda has supplanted abortion as the primary cultural point of contention between liberals and conservatives, but although that agenda is under earnest consideration by legislatures, religious bodies and educational institutions, its treatment by the dominant news media borders on an exclusive advocacy of the liberal point of view.

A recent *Newsweek* essay by Anna Quindlen exemplifies the problem. In her comments about gay civil unions in Vermont, and the Supreme Court decision about the Boy Scouts, she deplores anti-gay bigotry and homophobia, and concludes her article as she began it with scathing sarcasm directed at those who disagree with her.

The Quindlen assumption that no fair-minded person could conscientiously oppose the gay agenda is so widely shared by influential editors and commentators that much of the public never encounters the reasoning of analysts who are not bigots and are not motivated by fear or hatred in their concern about legalizing and normalizing same-sex relationships. As a result of this virtual blackout, gay issues are being decided by power struggles instead of by responsible efforts to find a rational accommodation for the conflict of valid principles.

John A. Howard

What is at issue is the eternal tension between the impulse to pursue one's own course and the necessity to modify one's conduct according to the requirements of group membership. This polarity is embedded in every organized endeavor, be it a kindergarten, a factory or a nation. As a group, each individual must observe certain restrictions on his behavior.

In a *smoothly functioning* free society, the citizens learn that lawfulness, truthfulness, honesty, respect for one's neighbors and many other informal norms of conduct must be observed in order for them to live and work together. They also learn that certain major social institutions are essential for community life including the courts, the press, the schools, the businesses and the families. If one of these institutions is incapacitated by corruption, shortsightedness or other affliction, the entire society is damaged.

The need to safeguard the institution of the natural family is what raises questions about the wisdom of carrying out the gay rights agenda. The late Congressman, Dr. Walter Judd, who had long been a medical missionary in China, used to give lectures stressing that it was the centrality of the family in Chinese living that provided the vitality and stability of the civilization which dated back thousands of years. The natural family—a man united to a woman in a lifelong covenant with responsibilities to older and younger generations—was held to be more important than all the other social institutions including even the government.

In sub-Saharan Africa, it was the natural family and the sexual mores undergirding it that used to provide effective protection against sexual pestilence. Last November at the World Congress of Families, Dr. Margaret Ogola, who heads a hospice for HIV-positive orphans in Kenya, spoke of the causes of the AIDS epidemic in black Africa. She said that for generations religious taboos had effectively repressed sexual activity outside marriage. Those tribal norms of sexual morality were shattered by Western influences—the mass marketing of contraceptives, the promulgation of value-neutral education and what she called "Planet Hollywood," which disseminates throughout the world the message that pleasure is the ultimate good.

In the United States, the statistics prove overwhelmingly that the

180

child raised by a father and a mother is far more likely, than children raised in other circumstances, to succeed in school, in a job and in a marriage, and is far less likely to have problems with crime, alcohol, illegal drugs, and emotional disorders.

The natural family is at the core of the Christian and Jewish faiths as it is in the Muslim faith, and as it was in the Chinese and African societies. In the blueprint for how people should live which God gave Moses on Mt. Sinai, The Ten Commandments specify how to safeguard the family. "Honor thy father and thy mother," (unmistakably a heterosexual family), sets forth the intergenerational obligations, and, "Thou shalt not commit adultery," is God's acknowledgment that the family is dependent on the observance of a code of sexual morality.

In the United States, the codes of sexual morality were woven into the culture and re-enforced by public praise and disapproval. Prior to World War II divorce was rare and deplored. Until 1964 the nation's colleges and universities still had regulations prohibiting the men from being in the women's dormitories after a certain hour, and vice versa, a long-standing policy acknowledgment of the society's public commitment to the ideal of premarital chastity.

There are religious, historical, sociological and psychological reasons to believe that the institution of the natural family and the sexual liberation movement, of which the gay rights agenda is a part, are mutually exclusive. The more there is of the one the less there will be of the other. If this hypothesis is judged valid, then the American people need to decide whether they deem it wise to sacrifice the natural family in order to accommodate the claims of gay rights. This is not a judgment to be made lightly, or to be decided by the urgent persuasion of advocates who have not done their homework.

Conceivably, accommodations could be found that provide a higher level of dignity and protection for sexual minority groups than has existed, without abandoning a national recognition that the natural family is the essential social unit of a viable society. That is a task for the wisest minds of the age.

CHAPTER XXIV

CONCLUDING OBSERVATIONS

November 2000

"How long will the American Republic endure?" This question was put to James Russell Lowell, the American scholar and diplomat, by the French statesman Francois Guizot. "The American Republic will last," replied Lowell, "as long as the ideas of the men who founded it remain dominant." Americans are no longer accustomed to thinking of ideas as the essential undergirding of their government. This is a crucial lapse.

The free society's dependence upon a specific set of ideas was tragically revealed after World War II. A number of African countries obtained their independence from colonial powers. After a few years, the supposition that these new nations had been freed from oppression faded. In a number of them, after an intense power struggle, a new regime took over that proved to be even more oppressive than the colonial one. These peoples had not grown up with a belief system that stressed the rights and the responsibilities of all citizens. Such standards of interhuman relationships cannot be easily infused into the value structure of a whole populace; they can only be operative when they have become the givens of daily living.

The American relinquishment of the belief system of the Founders began long ago, in the seed-bed of value-formation, the nation's educational system. Walter Lippmann, one of the preeminent twentieth century journalists, issued a scathing indictment of America's schools and colleges in a 1940 speech at the University of Pennsylvania. He charged them with ignorance of and damage to the society they were created to serve.

During the past thirty or forty years, those who are responsible for education have progressively removed from the curriculum of studies the western culture which produced the modern democratic state...

Modern education rejects and excludes...the whole religious tradition of the West...Thus there is an enormous vacuum...There is no common faith, no common body of principle, no common body of knowledge, no common moral and intellectual discipline. Yet the graduates of these modern schools are expected to form a civilized community. They are expected to govern themselves. They are expected to arrive by discussion at common purposes...

Having cut him off from the tradition of the past, modern education has isolated the individual. It has made him a careerist—without social connection—who must make his way—without benefit of man's wisdom—through a struggle in which there is no principle of order. This is the uprooted and incoherent modern free man.

Twenty-five years later, the eruption of radical activism, first at Berkeley, and then at universities throughout the nation revealed to a startled America a generation of students ignorant of the nature and importance of the institutions of their own society. Here were the cultural orphans anticipated by Lippmann. The "Student Movement" engaged in acts of opposition to the government, the military, the economic system, religion, the family, the laws and all the mores which prescribed proper conduct. The tablets of morality were wiped clean. Do-your-own-thing became the single respected norm.

Some college buildings were taken over. Others were burned. Library card catalogs were destroyed. Speakers were insulted and shouted down. Students defied the draft. At the University of Wisconsin, a laboratory bombing killed a faculty member. At Cornell University, the black militants, armed with guns, ordered the University President to sit on the floor of the auditorium stage until he was called upon.

In October of 1969, President Nixon appointed a panel of academic leaders to a White House Task Force on Priorities in Higher Education. President Hester of New York University served as chairman. Among the other fifteen members were the presidents of the University of Chicago, MIT, Vanderbilt, Tuskegee, Williams College and the University of Minnesota. I, too, was a member, possibly the only Republican college president they could identify.

Dr. Arthur Burns, at that time the President's Chief of Staff, gave us our charge at the White House. He said that the President was deeply concerned about the troubled campuses and wanted advice on how the U.S. Government could be helpful in reducing the turmoil and enabling the colleges and universities to carry forward their proper responsibilities without hindrance.

After several months of meetings, the Task Force assembled to consider the draft of its report to President Nixon. In that text and in the final report there was nothing to indicate any unusual difficulties on the campuses. There were recommendations for more federal funds for disadvantaged students, and Negro colleges, and health care professional education and two-year colleges. A new National Academy for Higher Education was proposed. The report urged colleges and universities to review their institutional purposes. These recommendations were found agreeable and sufficient by the other members.

I expressed concern that we were not addressing any of the aspects of campus turbulence cited by Dr. Burns. We needed guidance and help in protecting our premises from destruction. We needed to know what to do in response to bomb threats. We needed information about the purposes and plans of the revolutionary groups causing the campus strife. We needed Federal help in responding to the intense student hostility about the Viet Nam War. We needed official justifications for the U.S. involvement in Viet Nam. We had serious drug problems that required government help.

One of the committee members exclaimed, "But, John, all those matters involve value judgments!" I agreed. He said, "We can't take action involving value judgments." All the others agreed with him. For this representative group of eminent college and university leaders, value judgments had already become completely taboo. And that was thirty years ago.

The unilateral moral and spiritual disarmament that has taken place among colleges and universities has contaminated many aspects of daily living as these commentaries have noted. However, this rather dismal account of America's cultural trajectory tells only part of the story. In recent years, quite a number of counterforces have been created which offer hope for disengaging the nation from its thoughtless embrace of decadence. It is fitting that this volume should conclude with a glimpse of some of these centers of affirmation.

The urgent need to improve the formal education of the nation's young is widely acknowledged and many organizations are engaged in developing and trying to implement remedial programs. The one that most directly addresses the critical failing described by Walter Lippmann is the Home-Schooling Movement. It now serves an estimated 2,000,000 students and that number is growing by 15% a year. A study of 20,000 home-schooled students from 50 states found that they outperformed public and private school students in every subject at every grade level. Catholic, secular and Evangelical Christian publishing houses provide detailed curricula. A bi-monthly periodical, *Home-Schooling Today*, furnishes information about many dimensions of the home-schooling process and reports on the ever-multiplying support services available to parents and students. Two-thirds of the parents involved have chosen to engage in home-schooling in order that their children's education would reflect and reinforce the family's religious and cultural values.

Further information is available from The Home School Legal Defense Association, P.O. Box 3000, Purcellville, VA. 20134. Phone: 540-338-5600. Web site: www.hslda.org and from *Home Schooling Today*, P.O. Box 1608, Fort Collins, CO 80522-1608. Web site: www.homeschooltoday.com.

An organization that has moved surefootedly into the public schools' no man's land of morality is Project Reality. It has been a pioneer in the field of adolescent health education, teaching and evaluating abstinence-centered programs in the public schools since 1985. In 1999-2000 Project Reality reached 52,000 students in 350 Illinois schools. The organization's Reality Check rallies in Chicago and Rockford entertained and educated 30,000 students about abstinence from premarital sex and also from the use of drugs and alcohol. Reality Check is now a model for rallies throughout the nation.

Teacher symposiums, Power of Abstinence symposiums, and Reality Check rallies are scheduled for a number of states. A speaker's bureau is being mobilized that will feature young adults that include Miss America and Miss Black America Titleholders who are promoting abstinence as their particular platform issue.

For more information, contact, Project Reality, P.O. Box 97, Golf, Illinois, 60029-0097. Phone: 847-729-3298. Web site: www.projectreality.org.

In recent years the free speech zealots have commandeered the public square and purged it of prayer and overt references to the deity. Into this fervently defended void have quietly and adroitly moved Jim Russell and his Amy Foundation. First, he established the Amy Writing Awards which annually provide $34,000 in prizes to authors who, through articles printed in secular publications, make known biblical truths, reinforced with scriptural references. This journalism contest now attracts more than 1,000 entries. Winning commentaries have appeared in such periodicals as *Time, The Wall Street Journal*, and *The Washington Post* as well as in small town weeklies.

The success of this program led to the initiation of The Church Writing Group Ministry through which church members write letters to the editor providing biblical commentary about local or national issues. The letter writers are encouraged and educated through a bimonthly entitled *Pen and Sword.* Its text includes examples of published letters, columns and book reviews. There is now also an Amy Internet Syndicate which provides editorial page opinion columns free to any newspaper. The Syndicate columns, under the heading "Real Answers," are written by twenty authors who analyze current topics from a biblical perspective.

A new ministry of the Amy Foundation is now being developed, The Discipled Nation Plan Curriculum, designed to help church-going Christians move toward the full acceptance of Christ's teachings.

Contact the Amy Foundation, P.O. Box 16091, Lansing, MI 48901. Phone: 517-323-6233. Web site: www.amyfound.org.

Second to religious faith, no norm was of greater importance to the Founding Fathers than the adherence to the natural family— a man married to a woman bound by a life-long covenant, with responsibilities to their parents and their offspring. The same opinion-making forces that have marginalized public expressions of religious belief have so successfully stigmatized public support for the norm of the natural family that such support is scarcely found in current literature, entertainment and educational programs. In foreign countries as in America, the anti-family cultural output has led to the breakdown of marriage and all the tragic human consequences of that collapse.

The World Congress of Families was initiated in 1997 to bring together people and organizations to join in counteracting the powerful anti-family movement. In November of 1999, under the joint sponsorship of The Howard Center for Family, Religion and Society, and NGO Family Voice of Brigham Young University, 1600 delegates assembled in Geneva, Switzerland to participate in the Second World Congress of Families. They were Muslims, Mormons, Jews, Roman, Eastern, and Russian Orthodox Catholics, Evangelicals, Main-Line Protestants, African tribesmen and Native Americans, representing 275 organizations. A year earlier, the Planning Committee, drawn from the five inhabited continents, met in Rome, to reaffirm the definition of the natural family, determine the agenda and issue an invitation.

The opening plenary session took place in the Great Hall of the United Nations Building in Geneva. Dr. Allan Carlson of The Howard Center in Rockford, Illinois, gave the opening address. It was his vision and energy that had led to the creation of The Congress. He reminded the audience that fifty-one years earlier the United Nations had adopted the Universal Declaration of Human Rights. Among the provisions of that Declaration were: Article 12: No one shall be subjected to arbitrary interference with his privacy, family, home or correspondence; Article 16, 3: The family is the natural and fundamental group unit of society and is entitled to protection by the society and the State; and Article 26: Parents have a prior right to choose the kind of education that shall be given to their children.

During the course of the Congress, a number of the 103 eminent speakers told how various governments and societies had disregarded or repudiated these ideals with devastating consequences. Among the speakers were Mrs. Anwar Sadat, Cardinal Lopez Trujillo, President of the Pontifical Council on the Family, Francisco Tatad, former Majority Leader of the Philippine Senate, and Rabbi Daniel Lapin, President of Toward Tradition. At the conclusion of the conference, the delegates voted overwhelmingly in support of the Geneva Declaration which stated in part, "Free, secure and stable families that welcome children are necessary for a healthy society. The nation that abandons the natural family as a norm is destined for chaos and suffering."

At Geneva it was announced that prior to World Congress of Families III there will be regional assemblies held in Australia, France and Utah. A 6-part video tape is available which interviews speakers from the Geneva Congress on six key topics. All the Geneva speeches are also available on the Internet at www.worldcongress.org. Information is also available at The World Congress of Families, 934 N. Main Street, Rockford, Illinois, 61103. Phone: 815-964-5819.

In 1978, Alexander Solzhenitsyn gave the Commencement Address at Harvard. His title was " A World Split Apart." That division did not refer to the Communist nation and the free nations as one might have anticipated, but to the chasm between the materialistic, hedonistic, self-centered way of living and the ideals of the Christian heritage.

His concluding statement was:

Even if we are spared destruction by war, life will have to change in order not to perish on its own. We cannot avoid reassessing the fundamental definitions of life and human society. Is it true that man is above everything? Is there no Superior Spirit above him? Is it right that man's life and society's activities should be ruled by material expansion above all? Is it permissible to promote such expansion to the detriment of our integral spiritual life?

If the world has not approached its end, it has reached a major watershed in history, equal in importance to the turn from the

Middle Ages to the Renaissance. It will demand from us a spiritual blaze; we shall have to rise to a new height of vision, to a new level of life, where our physical nature will not be cursed, as in the Middle Ages, but even more importantly, our spiritual being will not be trampled upon, as in the Modern Era.

The ascension is similar to climbing onto the next anthropological stage. No one on earth has any other way left but—upward.